"The Alex Montoya Story redefines heroism."

> - Derrick Mayes
> Filmmaker and Producer

"Shows what faith and courage and tenacity can do."

> Rolf Benirschke
> President of RB Enterprises

"A hilarious yet touching story of love, struggle, and inspiration."

> Lidia S. Martinez
> Manager, Corporate Community Affairs
> Southwest Airlines Co.

"This book is a must read for anyone who has faced challenges or wishes to be inspired to greatness."

> Jim Ponder
> President / CEO
> Turnkey Strategic Relations, LLC

"Alex's style of writing is eloquent and the story he tells is inspiring. His positive attitude that *one person can make a difference* truly does make the difference. This story is nothing short of fascinating!"

> - Justin Tuck
> Notre Dame all-time sacks leader and defensive lineman
> for Super Bowl champion New York Giants

SWINGING *for the* FENCES

Keep Swinging!

Alex M

Keep Singing! ♡

[signature]

ALEX MONTOYA

SWINGING *for the* FENCES
Choosing to Live an Extraordinary Life

TATE PUBLISHING & *Enterprises*

Published by Tate Publishing & Enterprises, LLC
127 E. Trade Center Terrace | Mustang, Oklahoma 73064 USA
1.888.361.9473 | www.tatepublishing.com

Tate Publishing is committed to excellence in the publishing industry. The company reflects the philosophy established by the founders, based on Psalm 68:11,
"The Lord gave the word and great was the company of those who published it."

Published in the United States of America
ISBN: 978-1-60462-735-0
1. Biography and Autobiography: Specific Groups: Special Needs
2. Biography and Autobiography: Ethnic: General
3. Inspirational: Motivational: Biographical
08.11.17

ACKNOWLEDGEMENTS

In reading this book you'll see that a central theme is discovering how to make your dreams come true. It starts with realizing what is your passion and then dedicating your life to pursuing that.

The fact that you are reading this means I have realized one of my dreams. By the age of ten I had experienced enough unique, incredible, inexplicable things that I knew: *Someday I have to put this into a book.*

Because of my love for writing, I actually created certain chapters and stanzas as far back as 1992. But that's all they were, loose-leaf thoughts and stories, for over ten years.

In 2004 that all changed. While delivering a motivational presentation to San Diego County high school juniors at the Rotary Youth League Awards (RYLA) camp, one student turned the tables on me. *You've talked to us about going after your dreams,* he said, *but what dreams are you still pursuing?* It wasn't a question I expected, but two answers immediately came to mind: I wanted to work in Major League Baseball, and I wanted to publish a book.

After explaining that as a final answer to the assembled student leaders, I watched as they shuffled out of the large cabin that houses the annual RYLA camp. Just then a tall and thin gentleman with slightly graying hair approached me. He had to be 6'8" and smiled as he hunched over slightly to shake my hand. "Alex, my name is Jim Ponder," he said, "and here's my card. I think my company can do something about your book. Call me."

I did so, as soon as I reached my desk at the Hispanic Chamber of Commerce on Monday morning, and it was the greatest follow-up call I've ever made. So as I write these acknowledgements I will start with Jim Ponder, who made good on his promise to help. Actually he had less experience in publishing a book and had done more in the realm of promoting established authors, but after I met with Jim, shortly afterwards, I was sold. He exuded integrity, confidence, and a desire to put some good messages out there for people to read. "Take a chance on me, Pond," I told him, "and I'll take a chance on you."

We embarked on this pursuit together and learned great lessons in patience and determination. I wrote and Jim pitched—to publishers, editors, and potential investors who could help us in turning this manuscript into a published work. It was a long process, spanning nearly four years, and along the way we were rejected repeatedly.

But also along the way, we were eventually assisted by people to whom I am forever grateful. Irene Márquez rescued the manuscript when it was a collection of stories and jumbled thoughts and edited it to perfection. We spent months in her apartment outside downtown San Diego, writing and re-writing, proving her prose and patience are colossal. Bill Kuni, who you will read more about later, provided generous support to keep the project moving. Then Lidia Martinez and Southwest Airlines held a raffle for two plane tickets to help offset the publishing costs. Lidia is a mentor, encourager, coach, and dear friend.

Ultimately, there wouldn't have been the opportunity to publish had it not been for Tate Publishing in Mustang, Oklahoma. The day Dr. Richard Tate informed Jim and me he wanted his company to publish my book was a proud and joyous one. The constant direction and support I received from J.D. Byrum, Dave Dolphin, and Jesika Lay was incredible. Concurrently, I received unyielding support from Jim's company, Turnkey Strategic Relations in Escondido, CA as well as from his family, wife Carol and kids Garrett and Kelly. Thank you!

This book also would have been tough to complete without the urging of my lifelong mentors:

Robert Villarreal, formerly of the San Diego Hispanic Chamber, Bob Mundy at the University of Notre Dame, and Dave Nuffer of NST Communications. Thanks to Jen Laiber and Kathy Sullivan at Notre Dame, Peter Rowe of the *San Diego Union-Tribune,* and Peggy O'Leary and Rich Cellini of the University of San Francisco Master's in Sport Management Program. A writer cannot flourish without support and confidence from his employers, and I am blessed with great ones at the San Diego Padres: Jennifer Moores, Sandy Alderson, Jeff Overton, and Jenifer Barsell. My teammates at the Padres are phenomenal, and I am happy to report that a portion of the book sales will be donated to the Padres Foundation for Children and Friends of Scott Foundation.

Thank you for reviewing my book and providing insights, Tim Flannery, Rolf Benirschke, and Tony Gwynn.

Above all, thanks to God for this opportunity and all opportunities with which I have been blessed. Speaking of being blessed, beyond description, I am by my family: Mom and Dad for raising me and instilling sacred values; Grandma, Luis, Carlos, Ann Marie, Frankie, and all of our extended family. I love you all and have dedicated this book to you. I couldn't have done it without you.

Dedicated to my two mothers

FOREWORD

When I met Alex Montoya a decade ago, I did not grasp the severity of his disability.

Naturally, I noticed the poor guy's affliction. But it took years of observing him at close range—in auditoriums, accepting the cheers of admiring audiences; at the ballpark, cheering for his beloved Padres; in sports bars, cheering for his beloved Domers—to understand how this problem has warped his life.

Unfortunately, there's no cure. No therapy, no prayers, no sympathetic counsel has been enough to free Montoya from this cruel scourge:

He loves the music of the 1980s.

This is sad, yes, but it's also an outrage. When it comes to pop culture masterpieces, Montoya's '80s can't hold a Bic lighter to my '60s. Anyone who can't see that is disabled.

But what is a disability? When you get to know Montoya, you're forced to re-examine your notions about the less-than-able-bodied. On first glance, you'd have to say this guy is disabled. Severely dis-

TABLE OF CONTENTS

COLOMBIAN BEGINNINGS

Adversity comes in a myriad of forms: child-hood traumas, war, accidents—some obvious, others not. For me, though, amid the lush greenery and steep mountainsides of Colombia, hardship was present *when* I was born.

My misfortune was as noticeable as the heavy humidity draping over Medellin each summer. The doctors immediately reported it to my parents, Hernán and Ines. My father, a stout man, and his virtuous wife were stunned. What the doctors presented to them was as inexplicable as it was scary.

There were no predications of any difficulties during my mother's pregnancy, and my birth went smoothly. It, however, yielded some major surprises. On this June day in 1974, these particular health experts were flummoxed.

When born, I had no arms or a right leg.

Specifically, my arms were two stumps. My right leg was present but was only half the size of my left one. Every other aspect of my mother's delivery, as well as my other external and internal features, were fine.

The doctors found no reason for my missing three limbs. My father, given to heavily salted foods, certainly enjoyed his fair share of spirits. He drank the whiskey aptly named *Aguardiente*—known as "fire water," but my mother never drank. Neither smoked. My mom also did not take any dangerous medication, such as Thalidomide. This was taken by many expectant mothers in the 1960s, leading to their children being born as amputees. In fact, the only activity undertaken by my parents considered risky was this: they operated a home business constructing artificial Christmas trees, and the doctors wondered if pregnant Ines was exposed to some type of dangerous chemical. But the notion was like finding a needle in the haystack of one of the countryside *fincas*—farms.

"Don Hernán y Doña Ines," the doctor addressed my parents in formal titles, "we cannot explain why your son was born this way. Alejandro has a functioning heart and brain but only one complete limb. We may just wait to see if he makes it before presenting him to you."

Displaying instant passion and strength, Ines Montoya Gonzalez showed how even the most serene spirit can be riled up when it comes to defending one's child. "No!" she glared, "you will clean him up like you would any child. If he does not make it, then God will take him. Now bring him to me." In time, her words proved to be ironic because although I was taken to my mother, I was not destined to stay with her. God had His plan.

The doctors protested, but my mother was firm. I did indeed survive the tenuous first few hours, and everything, besides my surprising physical characteristics, was normal. Still, the doctors insisted on snapping as many photos and documenting as many notes as they could. In their minds, I was still at prohibitive risk of not surviving, and they wanted a record of this extraordinary birth with no explanation. And in the backs of their minds, no doubt was the question—even if I did, what quality of life could I enjoy?

Nonetheless, my home arrival was a joyous one. My brother, Jorge, and sister, Elizabeth, coddled their new younger sibling. All of my cousins did, and with my mother's eight siblings and my father coming from a large family, there were relatives everywhere. Although receiving nurturing care, there was also great worry.

Fear pervaded my family, and concern even gave way to anguish. Neighbors peered in to see if the story was true about the Montoyas bringing home a disfigured child. In Colombia, in that era, a baby with a disability meant a punishment from God for previous sins. Others did not assign such spiritual branding but still considered such a child to be a weakness. Often families shuttered away their hindered offspring, either out of spite or out of fear. Even those kind-hearted people who treated a child like any other could not mask this fact: this child would have no opportunity. Colombia in the 1970's was struggling economically, and jobs were sparse. Even able-bodied citizens did not find steady work. If disabled by birth or accident—in a country with no special education and limited medical resources— chances were, one would be prevented from going to school. With no education, how could one be gainfully employed, especially in a country already economically weakened?

That tormented my beloved Grandmother Fanny. She was my mother's mother and the family matriarch. *Abuelita* cast an imposing figure. This retired schoolteacher and mother of nine was generous, forthright, and, although strong, was deeply concerned.

One day, I am told, shortly after my homecoming my family gathered. We did not truly need any sort of reason to crank up the music, whip up a heaping of food, and snap up scores of pictures. But a new baby, disabled or otherwise, sure was a good excuse. As the mouth-watering *arepas* and *frijoles* were passed around and the family revelers belted out classic mariachi serenades, Grandma Fanny excused herself.

She slipped into one of the side bedrooms and stared out the window. Deep in thought, she was interrupted.

"Mamá, what is the matter?" It was her daughter Lucia, one of my mother's older sisters. Lucia resided in the United States but was visiting Colombia with her four offspring.

Grandma turned. "*Nada, m'ija,* go back and enjoy the party."

But my aunt Lucia persisted and finally Grandmother confessed. "I am worried for Alejandro. What will he do here? He can't go to school or get a job." Grandmother dropped her eyes. "He can't even play with the other children. He has no future. What will become of him?" My abuelita looked up. "Perhaps in the United States, but not here."

Upon hearing this, my aunt straightened her shoulders. "I am your daughter, and if you have taught me anything, it is this: If you spoil him and protect him and treat him with pity, he will become nothing. But if you treat him with love and respect and toughness and like every other child, he will become something great. If you want Alejandro to live a normal life, then treat him normally." Lucia took my grandmother's hand. "It would be great if he could live in America, but right now that's not possible. Treat him normally here and he will grow up to be what you raise him to be."

Unbeknownst to either one, my mother was standing nearby. She heard it all; the anguish and the firm statements. Ines stepped into the room and said thank you to my grandmother for her faithful concern and my aunt for reaffirming what my mother believed. Mother was committed to doing anything possible to ensure I lived a prosperous and productive life. But she also knew in Colombia that it would be challenging.

However, here I am. A college graduate and gainfully employed man. Obviously the doctors were incorrect asserting that I may not live, and my relatives and neighbors miscalculated that I would forever need "to be taken care of." So how did I get here? How did I go from the bleak prospect of a lifetime without education to a future brimming with promise?

Lucia and her four children returned to Northern California where her husband, Frank, awaited them. Approximately two years passed after the conversation between my grandmother and her daughter.

Frank, who served in the United States Marine Corps, also held a part-time job as a reserve police officer for the Vallejo Police Department. One particular foggy and damp evening, Frank was on his weekend beat assigned to patrol the grounds of a convention hall where a civic organization was hosting a meeting. Midway through the night, Officer Callahan slipped out a back door to enjoy his guilty pleasure—a smoke break. As soon as he reached into his carton, someone stumbled out right behind him.

"Evening, sir," the intruder intoned. "Got a light?"

Frank nodded and, before proceeding to light the fellow's cigarette, noticed a bizarre-shaped hat on the chap's head—cylindrical with an attached tassel. The gentleman wore a maroon jacket with Arabic-looking letters, gold-encrusted, near the pocket.

The stranger chuckled. "Noticing my jacket, are you? I'm a Shriner. The name's Harvey Fitzhugh."

At this he extended his right hand and, while shaking Frank's palm, continued on in a brogue, part-Irish and part-whiskey. "We're having a convention here. We do good work, you know, we take care of crippled children."

Bewildered, Frank inquired, "What do you mean, crippled?" He took a puff. "And how do you take care of them?"

"Well, maybe that term is changing, hell, I don't know." Harvey chortled. "But I do know we take all kinds of children—amputees, fire victims, handicapped kids—and help them. If they need prosthetics, plastic surgery, wheelchairs, we supply them. We own the Shriner's Hospitals for Crippled Children. Now don't get mad at me, that's the actual name."

Inhaling and exhaling through his nose (that always captivated me), Frank asked from where these children came.

"Oh, they come from all over the United States, needing surgeries and such. Even from Mexico and South America. That's what we do, give kids medical help. Free, all free."

Frank marveled but did not want to appear overly excited. He then offered, "Well, I have this nephew down in Colombia...my wife's sister's kid... and he's about two years old now." He drew another drag. "Well, he was born missing three of his limbs, and his family doesn't know *what* they're going to do. They say he seems bright, but they don't know how..."

Harvey dropped his Marlboro. "We can help him! We can help him! You get that kid to the United States and we have a hospital in San Francisco to take a look at him. If they see they can give him some artificial limbs or somethin', we'll take care of him—for free!"

"I don't know," Frank replied, squashing his cigarette underfoot, "let me talk to my wife and—"

Harvey again interrupted, "You gotta do this! You gotta!" He reached into his jacket pocket. "Here, I'll give you my card and here's my phone number. You get your nephew here and we can help him, I know we can!"

My uncle was cautious. After all, Harvey was still a stranger who reeked of Irish whiskey. Wasn't this all just a little too good to be true? Why was he so eager? Did the Shriners rely on good-work bribery to get into heaven?

He did accept Harvey's business card, though, and obliged the giddy old man's request of exchanging telephone numbers. Harvey Fitzhugh half-staggered, half-skipped back into the convention hall.

Imagine my uncle's surprise when the phone rang the next day. It was Harvey. He once again assured that if I could be flown to America, the Shriner's Hospital would give me a free medical assessment.

I do not know exactly all the details of the arrangements, but I suspect my mother's promise to make sure any and all opportunities available to me were foremost. Therefore, within a few months my family applied to obtain a visitor's visa.

My aunt and uncle paid for my mother and me to fly from Medellin to the Bay Area. Harvey's claims held substance as the Shriner's Hospital in San Francisco evaluated me and immediately fitted me for three prostheses. It meant an extended stay in their facility and time away from home, but they could help.

Harvey was ecstatic, as was my family in Colombia. They would miss me, but now chances for a productive life were greater than ever. Hence, my mother left me in the secure hands of her sister, her family, and Harvey the Shriner.

Soon I was given a walker to navigate a wooden "leg" and was fitted with two artificial arms—with hooks at the end. Quite the news in the neighborhood and my cousins took full advantage. They told nosy neighbors, "You know, he really can poke out your eyes!"

Proud Harvey the Shriner frequently roared on his motorcycle into Frank and Lucia's driveway in Vallejo, always ensuring his organization was handling all medical and living expenses. Proud of his success, he often took me to fundraising dinners where elderly women mussed my shaggy hair while pinching my chubby cheeks. And opened their purses.

It was apparent the United States held the most opportunity for me. So before long, a major family decision was made. I would live in the United States with my aunt and uncle—a great emotional sacrifice for my mother and a greater responsibility for her sister.

During this time, Frank also received transfer orders to San Diego. I was impervious to it all, since I was only four when both moves finalized. My focus was learning English and how to use my new contraptions, especially since one day a wheel from the walker got caught in a wooden plank on a deck, forcing my walker to capsize. I slammed into the ground, bled, and lost two teeth. The first of many falls. Slips. Other adversities.

Only later in life did I appreciate the supreme sacrifices made by my father and mother, her sister and husband, and offspring from both families. I also realized the value of Harvey's enthusiasm and persistence, plus the importance of believing in God and His unstoppable destiny for each of us.

COMING TO AMERICA

In 1978, the only thing I knew about my new country was the name "John Travolta." I struck *Saturday Night Fever* poses with my new arm and hook in the air, the other at my waist, and my leg turned outward.

We now lived in San Diego, where the sun shone daily amid an endless canopy of blue skies. In contrast, the challenges before me were less than sunny. And countless people—neighbors, relatives, anyone who examined the situation—reminded us: the road ahead would be severe.

How the heck would I handle all these new challenges? And if and when I did master the English tongue and utilization of my new prosthetics, I would always need to rely on society to "take care of me," wouldn't I?

Let me tell you what my parents had, as well as the Callahans: they had faith. My mother trusted God's decision of not only how I was born, but also whether I lived or died. The Callahans followed suit.

This is the first life principle I recommend when dealing with life's adversities:

Establish Your Faith

I believe you should center your faith in God, country, which I will discuss later, and yourself.

While some wondered if my disability was a divine punishment, my parents held steadfast to their belief that that was not the type of God they served. They had faith knowing God had a plan for my life, as He does for each of us, and it wasn't for me to waste away in helplessness. When I moved in with my aunt Lucia, who now took on the role of mother, she had an even greater revelation navigating my moral compass: God expects the most out of you. People ask if I thought the Lord created me this way "to teach others a lesson," or to serve that same purpose for myself.

"God doesn't create people to serve as reminders of anything," my new mama reminded me. "He is not cruel or mean or has anything to prove. He also does not care if you or anyone is born with greater limitations. He cares about what you *have*. When you live your life and see God in heaven someday, He's not going to judge you based on what you were missing, but instead on what you are *given*. You are missing some physical things, but He gave you a good mind and the ability to speak. What are you going to do with those?"

She also emphasized to me—and to my parents, who just made the incredibly selfless gesture of allowing me to move—that God does have a special caring for those born disabled. But He has sufficient power to move through *anyone* no matter our challenges. Whether one is an amputee, blind, deaf, rich, poor, educated, uneducated, it does not matter to God. He can make anyone's life extraordinary and—as we will see later—can display His power through any set of circumstances.

One has to have faith.

One afternoon my mother was preparing a favorite of mine—pork chops. However, before going into the kitchen, I had to dress. Ocean Pacific T-shirts were the rage then, and I needed to be cool. But first, I had to get it over my head because I *really* wanted to sit and eat that pork chop. After countless efforts, I gave up. That pork chop was getting cold.

"Why are you coming in here half-dressed?" she asked as I sauntered to the kitchen table. Mama didn't even glance up, which led me to wonder if she had eyes in the back of her head or sides. I later learned all children wonder and all mothers do.

"Because I can't get my shirt on."

"You what?"

"I ca—"

Before I said "ca" again, she looked up, raising one hand to the air.

"There's no such thing as 'can't,'" she proclaimed. "That word is not allowed in this household, especially when you haven't even given a full effort."

I lowered my head. This was cruel and unusual punishment, keeping a salivating boy from his pork chop.

"Look at me." Raising my head, I saw tenderness in her eyes, and in a clear voice, I heard, "You will always have challenges and limitations, but it's up to you whether they stop you or not." Wiping her hands on her apron, she encouraged. "Now go try some easier way to put on that shirt. If one doesn't work, try another. You'll think of something." She stroked my cheek. "Can't and faith cannot coexist.'"

Despite my young years, I felt—for lack of a better word—inspired. Returning to the bedroom, I picked up the T-shirt again. Once again turning my body into a pretzel, I attempted to squeeze into my OP shirt. Finally, it struck me. Instead of popping my head in first, as I'd seen others do, I slipped one prosthetic arm through a sleeve, followed by the other into the opposite sleeve. I stretched the shirt enough, allowing my head to glide through the center.

Pork chops and beans never tasted so good.

I had to believe I could do it. My mother believed, and she believed in God.

IT'S ALL ABOUT ATTITUDE

After you look up and realize God wants to empower you with a full life, you must determine what your attitude is going to be concerning yourself and your challenges.

Better than any Sesame Street parable, I was learning from my newfound mom, your attitude determines your altitude. As Mama also put it another time: "You didn't choose to be born missing your arms and legs. I didn't choose to be born with all four of mine. We didn't choose to be born in Colombia. No one chose to be born in America. We can't control these things. But there's only one thing in life we have complete control over—our attitude. Keeping a positive attitude is a choice we make impacting the rest of our days and lives."

Second life principle:

Choose Your Attitude

I thought about this on innumerable occasions and

marveled at both its simplicity, yet profound truth. There are countless books, seminars, and gurus out there ready to pinpoint the cause for one's unhappiness. They blame social environments, body image, overbearing parents, lack of parents, irresponsible parents, overly responsible parents, and more.

Though I am not one to doubt that your family, neighborhood, wealth, and relationships affect you, I am adamant they must not *define* you. Because for all the literature and wise sayings and seminars costing you a bundle (now *there's* something to be unhappy about), there remains this truth: happiness is a choice. And happiness is determined by attitude.

You choose your attitude, you choose whether to see the good or negative aspect in things, and you ultimately choose whether your life will be filled with pessimism and worry or optimism and happiness.

This not only negated any bitterness or self-pity I may have naturally generated (or believed from others), it gave me a renewed sense of hope. Also, I believe it guided my treatment of others. Often I would be skipping along somewhere in my bright yellow "San Diego Super Chargers" T-shirt and my corduroy shorts with knee-high socks, and inevitably stares and whispers followed. I would grow weary of those who approached me with questions or declarations such as, "Boy, do I feel sorry for you."

But when I viewed life through a more spiritual kaleidoscope, I felt more obligated to be patient. I believed God watched how I answered inquiries and how I treated people.

One of my responsibilities was to answer patiently and positively; besides, eventually I grew to appreciate when someone had the courage to ask me a curious question instead of pointing or coming to their own mistaken conclusions. In fact, I grew to wish all adults could be like children. Kids will never shy away from asking questions, and once their curiosity is satisfied, so are they.

We have to believe God's plan, and especially in this land of boundless opportunity, we can do anything we envision, but we must focus on attitude.

WORLD SERIOUS PADRES &
THE WONDER YEARS

Fostering your happiness relates to whom you choose to have around in your life. If you want fulfillment in terms of success and personal happiness, my next principle is:

Choose Your Friends and Mentors (Wisely)

When I was six and in the first grade, I was one of several students with physical disabilities who were part of a pilot program in San Diego. We were students at Albert Schweitzer Elementary, which was created exclusively for special education pupils. Right next to Schweitzer was Charles Lindbergh Elementary, with a chain-link fence directly separating the two.

I found it appropriate that Lindbergh was named after the famous pilot because I could see behind the fence at Schweitzer only non-disabled, or as we called them, "regular," kids. They just seemed to fly around. Nothing hampered them, not a wheelchair, crutch, or even slow gait. Yet I recognized they were kids just like us. The Lindbergh kids wore the same knee-high socks, terry-cloth polo shirts, long hair, elbow scrapes, and Velcro shoes. So why were they on one side of the fence, on a much larger playground, and we were on the other?

The following September a dozen or so of us were led to the other side of the fence, which was akin to Moses crossing the Red Sea. We were liberated, emancipated, and just glad to have a large backstop to play kickball. (Even the kids on crutches could play a mean game of kickball.)

We were placed in various classrooms, and it wasn't until years later I learned many teachers really didn't want us there. "Those kids belong in Special Ed," they objected. "We don't have time to be babysitters." This "mainstreaming" program, as it was known, was truly an experimental one. If we adapted to our new environment and the Lindbergh students would not shun us, our visitations would increase from once a week to more frequently, and eventually we would become full-time students there.

One cloudy day they led me back to the playground amid my new classmates. They wasted no time in asking questions about my two hooks or why I walked with a limp. Some were truly intrigued and gave me potato chips and fruit to test the finesse of my hooks. At the "elbow" joint of my prosthetic arms were two hollow holes. My friends found these holes particularly good for hiding candy. However, I had to be careful, because if I raised my arm to answer a question, all the sweets fell out. Those were the students who most often invited me to play with them. Others were more wary, because either I looked so different or they admitted they didn't want me to fall and injure myself.

This led to a group of about ten—one of us with hooks, nine without—to meet at that most sacred of playground institutions: the monkey bars.

Every kid played on the monkey bars, and I wanted to be no different. They climbed and hung and crossed and twisted their bodies into all kinds of entanglements. Amazing the types of laughter and shrieks metallic bars elicit.

When I expressed my interest in scaling the metal ladder, half the group scoffed. Some were outright teasing, saying there was no way I could latch my hooks onto the slippery bars. Others doubted, yet they were more concerned that I may lose grip and tumble to the ground. The remaining four or so companions smiled and encouraged, "Well, if you try we're right here to support—or catch—you."

One stepped up: a wiry little girl wearing a pleated skirt and matching red ribbon in her hair. It was my friend Margarita, whom I recall taking a liking to because she shared the same name as my aunt in Colombia. Her family came from the Philippines, and her mother, an in-class volunteer, used to pick me off the floor by one arm just like a rag doll. She also made the most delicious rolled lumpia.

Margarita had big, chocolate brown eyes, short midnight black hair, and when she spoke, her tone was soft, but the impact was not.

"Alex, don't listen to these guys," she stated. "You can do it. If you think you can climb up those monkey bars, then you can. If you never try, you'll never know. If you fall, you'll land on the sand, but we'll even stand below you to make sure that doesn't happen. You've never tried this before, but I want to see you give it a shot. I believe in you."

Pretty heady stuff for a first grader, huh?

And for me, climbing these bars was the 1980 Super Bowl, World Series, *and* season finale of "Dallas."

I decided to reward Marga's confidence and began the slow ascent on the bars. Inch by inch, I struggled up the ladder before coaxing myself about halfway across the horizontal grid. What seemed like leagues below my dangling feet were my supporters and detractors. Once I made it up there, however, even the ones who said I couldn't accomplish this were yelling their support as boisterously as Margarita.

The cheers continued, and I felt empowered, felt I could do anything. I was above the ground and at the height of my bliss.

Suddenly, an ominous sound blared across the playground. It was sudden and piercing, and its impact was instant.

BAAAAAAAAAAAAAHHHHHHHHH-HHNNNNNNNNNNKKKKKK.

The sound all playground revelers despised: the school bell, indicating recess was over. We must've had a worn-down battery in ours because it was less of a bell and more like an alarm clock buzz.

Suddenly, I felt like Moses because, underneath me, the Red Sea parted again. All of the kids, even my buddy Marga, ran off in different yet equally hasty directions. It was just me, clamped onto the monkey bars.

What I failed to mention was this was a particularly cold day. It was cloudy. And windy, extremely windy. Picturesque San Diego, which normally has blooming blue skies and balmy temperatures hovering near 72, suddenly turned frigid as the wind picked up its force. In all actuality, they were probably just harmless seaside breezes, but when you're six and alone on a metal ladder, it's a gale force.

Just when I thought I was doomed to an eternity on an isolated playground, a voice bellowed from behind me. I recognized instantly it was my teacher, and simultaneously she was not happy. This I could tell because when she called out my name, she used my *entire* name.

"Alejandro Montoya Gonzalez! Recess is over! What on earth are you doing?"

"Oh, nothing." I noticed how much her bellbottoms were flapping due to the wind. "I guess you could say I'm just...well...hanging around."

At this she tried unsuccessfully to hide a smile, repressing it with a forced frown, but I could hear her chuckling as she dismounted me from the monkey bars.

Besides learning humor can sometimes diffuse a tense situation, I learned a lot that day, even at six years old. I learned you never know what you can accomplish until you try it. That listening to either naysayer or your own fears guarantees failure. Failure is *not* trying.

Having friends help you flourish is crucial, but it's also possible to have great friends and not get too far in life. In order to truly grow and have an example of a life, it is imperative to have a mentor.

Your mentor can be a teacher, coach, pastor, instructor, counselor, or simply someone in a specific career you wish to follow.

This is not intended merely for students or young professionals. I encourage even those established to constantly look for someone older than them who can impart wisdom. Because life is a series of transitions, it is immeasurably helpful to have someone to show you how they did it. This holds true for questions you will have professionally, spiritually, and personally.

Your mentor can be your cheerleader and your sternest critic. It should be someone who has attained a level of success you aim to reach so they can lay out a path for you to follow. They should have personal experience overcoming their challenges and frustrations to help you face yours.

Mentors can also be of critical help in steering you down a certain path. In my life, I have been blessed with a multitude of mentors at various points, each of them offering guidance pertinent to that period but with lasting influence.

Two teachers come to mind, Mrs. Peggy Whitmore and Mrs. Irene Negus.

The former was the resource teacher who assisted us Schweitzer students with the transition to Lindbergh and served as the liaison for other teachers dealing with the difficulties of helping us mainstream.

Mrs. Whitmore quoted poetry, literature, and classic theatre, yet never appeared highbrow. She knew of my precocious nature.

One afternoon, Mrs. Whitmore cornered me and asked, "Alex, what is this I hear about you chasing girls?"

Shrugging my shoulders, I replied, "Just having fun."

"Yes, I understand, but does that mean you have to pinch them—in the butt!"

By this time, I had learned how to delicately use my metal hooks to do no real harm.

Busted.

"You need to promise me you are going to behave." She extended her hand. "Let's shake on it."

"You've got a deal." As I raised my right arm, streams of Snickers, Goodbars, and Hersheys tumbled out of my arm "holes."

Busted again.

Mrs. Whitmore developed a program fostering reciprocal understanding. One day each week, when our grammar school ended at noon, she had the former special education students cook and serve a meal for teachers, followed by ample social time. It served as a reminder to the teachers not to underestimate our abilities while allowing them to vent their frustrations and concerns.

The whole "disabled-students-as-restaurateurs" experiment worked so well in 1980, the teachers at Lindbergh allowed us into their classrooms, and by 1982, there was a waiting list of teachers wanting *more* students with disabilities. (This was such a groundbreaking occurrence that the local PBS affiliate developed a documentary.)

One of the instructors supportive from the outset was Mrs. Negus, who in 1984 invited me to be a part of her Gifted and Talented Education (GATE) curriculum. I had experienced this advanced type of class the previous two years, but admittance into Negus's high-level program was not guaranteed. She had to approve of each student's participation, as she did with me—with one important caveat.

"Young man," she said in a shrill, yet dignified manner, "in my class there are no shortcuts. I believe you have immense potential and can succeed in my class. But it won't be because I take it easy on you, as others may have."

She was right. I had experiences where some teachers may not have pushed me as hard as they did other students out of well intentioned but misguided sympathy. In fact, at times she pushed me harder than her other pupils, perhaps trying to reinforce her high expectations.

What made it additionally harder was not only that her class was taxing, but I also could not enjoy playing baseball, basketball, or other sports. And in school, it seemed everyone played some sport, which was an outlet for the students to take their mind off schoolwork. And when the Padres played in their first World Series in 1984, I was enraptured and vicariously shared their victory along with the rest of San Diego. That's when a dream began—but I am ahead of myself.

Needless to say, given my physical disabilities, I knew I would never play sports requiring the use of hands. It was frustrating.

However, Mrs. Negus, sensing my longing, but not one to coddle, said, "Young man, you do have other abilities. With your glib manner, you can announce the games." My reputation for chatting preceded me, for she added, "I know you will do it cleverly. And then you can write about it."

It was an epiphany! I could do something! In sports! I did have a strong voice and knack for putting together catch phrases to describe the action. So while my friends were running up and down the court, I'd often be the play-by-play guy for the spectators: "Milsap takes the ball and gets ready to shoot over Lumpy. Here's the shot…it's gooood! Stick a fork in Lumpy and his team because they are done!"

All the talking served well on the court but cost me in the classroom. Sacred activities were denied—recess, a field trip once, and the chance to enter a creative writing contest.

That last denial hit home—hard. Although I did not realize it, writing had become one of my favorite activities, but I didn't appreciate its significance. I only knew not entering the writing contest wounded me. So, it made little sense when Mrs. Negus said, "Trust me, this hurts me more than it hurts you."

Until I saw the wisdom in her punishment. You

see, the reason Mrs. Negus became a mentor was this: she knew its impact. A few days later, after Margarita, Dusty, Lesley, and Hope—the 1980s spawned great childhood names—had submitted their essays, Mrs. Negus called me to her desk after school.

Noting how disappointed I looked due to missing the contest and my chitchatting being the culprit, I thought she was going to berate me. Instead, she had a more cogent point, "Young man, you are a good writer. I've seen your work."

It was true. Thinking back, my essays, papers, and reports all earned A's. However, writing to me was heretofore a leisurely activity, something to offset my terrible math grades.

Mrs. Negus continued, "You were sad about missing the contest because it's important to you."

I nodded with downcast eyes.

Lifting my chin with her fingertips, she continued, "People don't miss something unless they value it." She put her hand on my shoulder. "Writing is important to you because you are good at it. You are a writer. Now value it and don't squander your talent."

A light bulb, fireworks, and clap of thunder all turned on, exploded, and struck. Mrs. Negus assigned meaning and lit a fire within me, which was never extinguished.

Funny how teachers have the ability to do that like few other professions.

Mrs. Whitmore and Mrs. Negus continued to encourage me. The two of them decided one day—perhaps they met in the lunchroom plotting how to further confuse, yet motivate me—I should run for sixth grade class president. I thought the two ladies had perhaps gotten on the monkey bars themselves and fell on their heads. I had a great deal of friends within my classroom, but to the general campus, I still often felt ostracized. I was the kid with hooks and a limp and big glasses and often saw kids pointing and whispering. Why would they want to elect me president and want to hear what I had to say about proposed bans on dodgeball and the dearth of bake sales?

Which was the two teachers' point exactly. The students still saw us as different. Some poked fun, others wanted to avoid contact, but seldom were we treated as peers.

We agreed on a silly and exploitative theme, "Get Hooked on Alex Montoya," as a campaign slogan. Then, despite the fact that I could talk, listen, and even laugh, students still saw me as a freak. It may sound sublime, but even in the mid-80s if you were not accustomed to having a person with a disability in your midst, you were not used to them being a regular person. That's what the students themselves told me. After that, they wanted to know how I was going to save dodgeball.

In the end, I lost the election to someone with far better hairspray usage and a more detailed plan for preserving our violent-yet-cherished sport (which was eventually banned two years later). But I proved to the students that the kids they had regarded as different were just like them. In the process, I also proved to myself with determination and unflagging spirit that I could do things I hadn't thought possible. The monkey bars in first grade, becoming a writer in fifth grade, and running for "office" in sixth all taught me the value and necessity of surrounding oneself with supportive friends and challenging mentors. I learned that in order to succeed you must surround yourself with those who want to see you succeed. Not that they should avoid providing constructive criticism or risk warnings—a true friend always looks out for one's best interests—but your friends should help you flourish. Surround yourself with friends, colleagues, and family members who are as happy for your success as they are about theirs. Other mentors followed, as you will read, with as much significance, but the first were Mrs. Whitmore and Mrs. Negus. And I thank them every time we exchange emails or I see them for lunch.

THE GREAT AUDITION

As important as it is to believe in yourself, a point will come when you will ask yourself why you are doing this. Is our primary goal in life to attain wealth and fame? What if we achieve our wildest dreams—what then? Or what if we do not have lofty ambitions beyond making a comfortable living and raising a family? Is that so wrong?

Countless philosophers ponder the meaning of life, each of them straining to explain reasons for our existence and what we are intended to accomplish on earth. That, of course, delves into religion, philosophy, psychology, and is rooted in a question that many still ask today: *what is the meaning of life?*

If this book can answer that question, then stick a fork in me because I am *done,* retired, and complete, with nothing more to write. Not only will I not pretend to have the answer to the question, but also I am glad to not know. Life would lose all its meaning if we knew the exact purpose and ending.

What matters is not the final answer or destination, but the journey.

I believe God is pleased whether we choose to reach unattainable heights or live a quiet, family-centered life. I am convinced whichever path you choose, He cares more about how you go about it and how you treat people along the way.

In the case of personal achievement, I look at life under the phrase of what I call *The Great Audition*. We all have a limited amount of time to show God what it is we're doing with our lives. Again, the object is not necessarily to see who can acquire the most material wealth or who has the greatest prestige, fame, and worldly possessions.

What God wants to see in this *Great Audition* is simply what we did with the gifts. God gave us all specific talents, gifts, desires, and opportunities. He even placed certain key people in our lives. When the day arrives our time on earth is finished, He will want to know what we did with those. If He gave you an incredible gift with athletics, science, or singing, did you maximize or squander them? If He presented you with encouraging parents or a teacher who was excited to help you in improving a skill, how did you treat them?

In my case, I can tell you that God will not care one bit about what I am missing. I'm a triple amputee, so what? He knew I would be born this way even before my parents did. Not that He is devoid of compassion or caring, of course. God is Love. But instead of having a level of pity or reduced standards because of my disability—and the same applies for those who acquire their disability later in life—He is going to want to know about what I *had,* not what I was lacking.

What did I do with the ability He gave me to write, speak, and climb monkey bars? What did I do with the fact He gave me the two most incredible mothers, in Medellin and San Diego, who made countless sacrifices so I could succeed?

Also, what did I do with the obstacles and adversity He put in my path? Did I let it defeat me or make me stronger? In God's eyes, adversity is as much of an opportunity as so-called advantages can be. It makes you tougher, stronger, and far more solid in character.

That's what God's going to want to see in my life. Every day for all of us is like one big audition. And I don't want to blow it. That is what drives me—every day.

Beyond that, though, there is a larger purpose for all of us. It should drive us no matter where we are and should be a recurring theme during each point and place of our lives. My next principal:

Make It Better

Whether it is your school, work, church, organization, or even a personal relationship, you have the ability to improve it so that it is appreciably better than when you first arrived. Even the relationships that are a part of this process will inevitably be touched.

Though we all desire stability in our lives, we know there are some places we will inhabit for just a short time. It is expected, on the average, you will attend a minimum of three schools as you grow up and perhaps college. If you matriculate at a university, whether you graduate at age 22 or 72, you expect to leave. We know we are only there for a certain number of years. This also holds true in the workplace, especially in today's economy, where it is not unusual to stay at a job for approximately two years and then seek a new opportunity. Even if someone stays with the same employer for 30–40 years, rare is the case where that occupation is the person's first— or even last.

We're always on the move; change is inevitable. Thus, the opportunities for us to impact our environment—an environment that, chances are, we will be leaving at some point—are strong. Everywhere you travel in life, literally and figuratively, there is an opportunity to make it better so your impact is felt long after you have gone.

Allow me to provide two personal illustrations of this principle.

When I was in high school, I coined a new word for "handicapped," a word I disdained because it is derived from an Old English term describing people who were cap-in-hand, i.e. beggars. I used handi-*capable*. Because regardless of our disabilities, many of us are just as capable as "normal" people. It was an unfair label, which by nature unjustly segregates and tempts discrimination. The more accurate word caught on, and soon the San Diego section of the *Los Angeles Times* did a story on my new usage. In time, however, "people with disabilities" or "physically challenged" became a more accurate term. But for that period of time, a paradigm shifted.

Thus, when I went to a human relations/diversity camp in Flagstaff, Arizona, the summer after my junior year, I was spoiled. I expected everyone would accept me and be especially welcoming of this bold, new term I introduced.

Not so. The camp was sponsored by a national organization called the National Conference of Christians and Jews (NCCJ) (which has since changed the final two words to Community & Justice). Their aim was to underscore how historically rival groups can come together when those groups learn about what unites, not divides, them.

I was excited about a week of hiking, recreation,

and learning about other cultures. I knew there would be some imposing challenges like the rugged hills between each cabin and the sweltering heat, which would drain me. But I had complete confidence that I could "get by with a little help from my friends," as the old song goes.

On the first day of this weeklong excursion, I prepared to check in with the other 300 campers who assembled from Southern California, Nevada, and Arizona. We were all high school students, and naturally, there were more than a few stares and points in my direction, but I wasn't unnerved by them. If staring were the worst thing I'd face all week, things would be fine once they got to know me, right?

Suddenly, a barrel-chested man with black curly hair and sunglasses straight out of *The Godfather* collection approached me. I recognized him as the camp director who gave a powerful oration on why this was called Camp Anytown because we were learning to combat prejudices and stereotypes found in any town, any city, and any neighborhood across America.

Eager to meet him, I stuck out my hook to shake his hand and nearly deflated the bulging potbelly protruding from his Izod shirt.

Imagine my shock then when I heard his first words, "Son, you don't belong here."

Oh, was I in the wrong line? Was I supposed to

turn in my sleeping bag first, or perhaps there was a separate line for all handsome guys with oversized glasses?

That was not the case. The head counselor continued, "We've never had a handicapped student here. I had no idea you were, uh...well...as you are. And if I had known, I woulda never let you come here. There's too much liability, and I don't have time to babysit you. Now the other counselors told me I can't send you home, so we're stuck with you. Just don't expect any special treatment, you hear?"

My emotions were anger mixed with shock blended with fear. The kind that sticks your heart in your throat and makes your flesh burn.

Honestly, I don't recall how I responded. I'm sure my lip quivered and I felt ashamed knowing peers nearby witnessed this humiliating exchange. I know also that, although I am a short guy to begin with, I felt about two feet tall at that moment.

There must not have been any clever retort on my behalf, or even some sort of pleading or words reassuring him I would require no "special treatment," because I don't remember him saying anything more.

I just remember feeling hurt.

And then going through a splendid week of camp. As expected, I made friends, met several girls I was convinced were destined to be my wife, answered daily questions about my arms and leg, and, like the rest of the campers, enjoyed the profound experiences of this life-changing camp. Sure enough, the dusty hills, steep inclines, and staggering heat were formidable, but nothing unconquerable. I was delighted to see how many campers and counselors—except the Godfather, who maintained his distance all week—offered help at every turn, and they learned sometimes I accepted and other times I chose to handle tasks independently.

By about the fourth day I knew I survived the physically challenging aspects of this camp. Whenever I saw the Godfather, I wanted to flaunt my success in front of him, to tell him maybe he should be the one looking for a "babysitter."

But I knew it wouldn't be right.

Likewise, when I saw one of the harsher elements of Camp Anytown was to segregate the kids according to ethnicity, religion, or wealth—a painful but important exercise to underscore how we do this in life every day, often unknowingly—I saw an added element of hypocrisy. How could the head counselor be so devoted to the cause of bringing people together, yet intentionally want to exclude me? Sure, he noted liability was a concern, but how could he be so sure I'd fall and become injured and want to sue? He let his fears take over his thinking, the very antithesis of this camp, and I wanted to hurl several angry verbal volleys in his direction.

But again, it just did not feel right.

When the last day arrived, there were plenty of tears and even more hugs. I felt personally satisfied that I survived both the rugged emotions and rough terrain of the camp. I also decided to merely smile and nod at the Godfather, leaving things positive. And let him go back to Vegas, Atlantic City...wherever it is Godfathers go.

Suddenly, as I finished saying "Call me" to one of my future wives, I felt a hand on my shoulder. I turned and...cue the dramatic Italian music...it was the Godfather.

His hair was still curly, the belly still bulging, and those darn sunglasses were way too big and overloaded with rhinestones. But this time his expression was different. Gone was the menacing scowl, suddenly replaced by a pensive look, and then trickling down his cheek...was that a *tear?* I've seen all the mob movies, Godfathers don't cry! There's no crying in the mafia!

"Son," he said to me while removing his shades, "I was wrong, very wrong. As soon as I saw you step off that bus, all I could think about was the problems you may cause. I figured you'd need extra help, or get hurt, or really screw up my camp, youknowwhatI'msayin'?"

I nodded, perhaps still in shock.

Godfather continued, "It didn't take long for me to realize you wasn't a problem. You licked this camp. And I fully expected you to come up to me and tell me to go stick it. But you didn't, and I admire that. Not only that, you changed my thinking. I used to tell the camp organizers I didn't want any handicappers 'cause they'd be nothin' but a pain. Well, someone snuck you in, I don't know who. And I thank you; from now on, I want *more* disabled kids here. All's I can say is you changed my way of thinking. Please forgive me."

I gave the Godfather a tight hug and thanked him for being so open with me. He then muttered something about calling him if I needed anything "handled," I'm not sure. But we parted and I felt not only satisfied, but redeemed.

I did not attend Camp Anytown expecting to change it, no more than I do waking up each morning expecting to change the world. I just got up as you do, except one leg at time, literally. I looked to have fun, learn something new, and go about my business. If someone learned a new lesson from me, then wonderful.

But what I failed to see is the power we each possess. I happened to change that camp quite accidentally, as I was just being a teenager and having fun. But I also knew there was something imperative about maintaining an upbeat attitude, and taking the higher road, when I just as easily could have been rude or spiteful to the head counselor.

Really, I didn't see the power I had, and the opportunity, to truly improve my surroundings. I am fortunate Camp Anytown became more inclusive and hospitable to *all* kids just by some of the things the staff and campers learned from watching me; like when to offer help and when to stop worrying one's challenges may impede them.

But truly, we all have this opportunity wherever we are! Look around at your current surroundings. Examine your workplace, school, and groups to which you belong. What areas are lacking? What can be improved? What will be more efficient or whose life can you improve if you decide to step up and take on an added responsibility?

Make the commitment and you will always be remembered as the person who impacted a place, and made it better.

DEPORTATION OR DEGREE?

Just like attitude is a choice, so is the direction of your life. Few, if any, stumble onto greatness. It's a choice, not a chance. There are always several factors involved, like timing, and knowing the right people. I am a huge believer in the power of networking. However, none of those should be confused with luck. I believe in blessings and hard work. Good fortune is a break or two going your way, but usually brought upon by putting yourself in position to succeed. Don't rely on fate to determine your happiness and don't curse bad luck when adversity comes your way.

If you want to succeed, make it a stated choice. Then state your ambition because you are choosing to live an extraordinary life. This will mean different things to different people. Some dream of being rich, famous, or powerful, while others find greatness in establishing a solid career and raising a peaceful family. Whatever your definition of extraordinary, be determined to pursue that life. Then develop a plan of how to get there and seek more mentors who will help you in your journey.

Don't Just Live Life, Choose To Live An Extraordinary Life

One of my childhood dreams was to go to college, in particular the University of Notre Dame. To my dismay, some high school friends and guidance counselors opined it was an overly ambitious destination. Notre Dame was far away (South Bend, Indiana), academically prestigious (highly ranked by most education publications), and expensive (you could buy a luxury car for what one-year's tuition costs). Frankly, their concerns were not entirely incorrect. It was indeed far, and frigid, and pricey, and my grades were good, but Notre Dame was looking for students with sterling grades.

However, there are some places you feel a calling toward, and for me it was Notre Dame. Above all, it emphasized spirituality and was not bashful about doing so. I also wanted to experience life outside of the California paradise and see different weather and lifestyle. Part of that lifestyle was to go where sports were not just an activity, but a passion.

I was familiar with the fervor of Fighting Irish athletics. As a ninth-grader, I followed their football team's 1988 national championship and was impressed at the school's unrelenting team spirit.

But it went far beyond touchdowns and trophies. I noticed the vigor of the student-athletes and fans and their undying loyalty to the school. Ivy-covered walls, crinkling leaves, crisp autumn afternoons in Indiana...it was my idea of what college should be like. So I made a conscious and single-minded choice to live an extraordinary life and matriculated to Notre Dame.

I wrote my personal statement—with which I was confident because what I lacked in math I regained in written skills. When I was 14, I started that necessary evil known to the male species as shaving. Clearly, holding a razor appeared difficult at best. Thus with the help of my mom I developed a technique. I sat in the bathtub with a small rounded mirror placed on the floor. On the edge of the tub, I set the can of shaving cream. With my left limb, (I didn't use my prosthetics) I squeezed out shaving cream and applied it to my face with my right limb. Cradling the razor blade between my toes on my left foot, I crouched over and shaved. I became proficient, except for once—still bear the scar on my left cheek.

My essay was simply entitled "I Can Shave with My Left Foot."

In applying to my dream school I focused on what I had, not on what I may have been missing. I knew I could give Notre Dame a videotape, a love for writing, and a story I knew would be pretty tough to replicate.

I must admit, though, once I discovered the wonders of electric razors, which were easier to hold and provided less nicks and cuts, I started shaving with my hooks instead of my left foot. Besides, by my junior year of college I had another hindrance, my rapidly expanding belly, making it a little less comfortable to be hunched over. But I digress.

I chose three perceived tiers of potential colleges: a long shot or dream school, some attractive and sensible schools, and at least one safer choice. Thus I spent my holidays stuffing mailboxes with applications. After months of tortured waiting, spring arrived and with it so did letters from various colleges. I smiled whenever a large packet with an institution's embossed logo reached my house. The ones ready to welcome me were UC Berkeley, UC Santa Barbara, Boston College, and Boston University.

One rainy April evening, I came home with only my brother Frankie in the house. Frankie has Down Syndrome and is a hero to me because of his enthusiasm, caring, and boundless love. He shared my dream, looking over my shoulder when I opened college letters. So he took immediate interest when I came inside with two envelopes in my hand.

"Is it, is it?" His eyes shined.

Noticing the Duke University return address,

whose basketball team just so happened to be on the TV screen in the living room playing for a national championship, I tore it open. I read the words, "We regret to inform you...",

"Is it, is it?" Frankie asked.

I tossed the letter aside. "No!" I must admit to a "sour grapes" attitude vowing to never root for the Blue Devils ever again.

"Come on, Alex, open the other one."

It was then that I recognized the gold ND in the upper left-hand corner. My trembling was matched with fear, because the envelope was small and skinny. Other schools sent large envelopes as welcome packets—and slender envelopes for rejection letters.

My heart pounded and I remember my mouth feeling dry. I handed it over to Frankie.

"Here you open it." I wondered...what if they rejected me...what if this dream does not come true...what will I do...what then...

Frankie grabbed the letter and tore open the seal. With a hopeful smile, he handed it to me.

With trembling hands, I unfolded the sheet. And I heard myself whisper, "Dear Alejandro...we are pleased..." Pleased? Pleased? Yes! Pleased! I bellowed "*that you have been accepted to the University of Notre Dame...*" Dropping the letter, I screamed, scared the family cat, grabbed Frankie, whose eyes watered as he yelled, "*All right!*"

We high-fived over and over again and in honor of the Fighting Irish, I taught Frankie how to dance an Irish jig. I achieved a dream! One some stated was beyond my grasp.

I was going to *The* University of Notre Dame.

I would like to say that the final two months of high school were full of bliss, but truthfully, they were anxiety-ridden. The visa allowing me to come to the United States at age four had expired, and my family heard the government did not grant immigration amnesty to people with disabilities. The thinking was that the government needed to take care of us. It turns out that it was false advice and we lost valuable time keeping my expired visa status a secret.

The previous summer at a two-week journalism camp at San Diego State University, I met a reporter for the *San Diego Union-Tribune* named Fred Alvarez. We became quick friends having writing in common. At prom time during my senior semester, he thought it would be fascinating to do a story on how a guy with two hooks prepares for the dance. I didn't see why it was so compelling, but it did give me another idea.

"Fred," I approached him one afternoon. "What about a real human interest story?"

"What do you have in mind?" He took out his pen and pad.

I gave him a quick overview: Colombian immigrant overcomes some tough odds, gets into a prestigious university, but there are scholarships issues and will now face an immigration judge who will make his Notre Dame dream come true or be shipped to his native country, which now is foreign to him.

Fred still liked the prom story better, but my powers of persuasion prevailed and he reluctantly agreed. He submitted the article to his editors. He was as stunned as I was when the *San Diego Union-Tribune* placed it on the front page the following Sunday.

Unbeknownst to us, this would get me to Notre Dame.

(Fred eventually became a journalist for the *Los Angles Times*. I am still waiting for the finder's check, but that's my opinion.)

Less than a week later was when I fully saw the power of extraordinary dreaming and the further impact of mentorship. As I prepared for my final month before graduating from San Diego High School, a school in the heart of the city where downtown buildings cast their shadows on the campus, I met Bill Kuni.

He read the article in the *San Diego Union-Tribune* detailing my visa expiration and how I was relying on an immigration judge to grant me legal residency in order to accept the college scholarship offers—including the one from Notre Dame.

Bill had sold his knee-brace company and part of his vision of living an extraordinary life was not just being a successful businessman and venture capitalist. He also started funding scholarships to help youths pursue extraordinary lives.

After reading Fred's eloquent prose, Bill marched right into San Diego High and asked the principal if he could meet me. When I was summoned to the principal's office, completely unaware of why I was being pulled from dreadful Geometry class, I figured maybe I was being punished for that excessive talking which never quite went away from the Mrs. Negus' days.

I walked in just as he was waving the newspaper article in front of my principal, Dr. Amparan, shouting, "Is this all true? Does this kid go here?" Bill continued, "Where is he? I need to talk to him! Need to tell him never to give up."

"Tell him yourself," Dr. Amparan said, pointing to me, as I stood bewildered in the doorway.

Bill stepped up right to me, shook my hook as he had been doing it all his life, then patted my back so hard I stumbled forward. He was tall, an affable fellow with not much hair, a slight Texan accent and a grin to match.

"This all true?" He shook the newspaper.

"Yes, sir." I swallowed. "It is."

"Well, you know what I am going to do?"

It was hard telling, but I hoped to God Dr. Amparan would intervene if necessary.

"Young man, my name is Bill Kuni. And someone like you deserves help."

Now Kuni was pronounced "que-nee," which rhymed with loony, which I thought he was after I heard what he planned to do with a kid he didn't even know.

"Young man, we are going to get you to Notre Dame and I am the man to do it." He looked me straight in the eye. "I will make arrangements to get you a scholarship."

There are times in your life when your breath is taken away and once you exhale, your body reacts. Mine was by throwing up my arms, hooks and all into the air.

Kuni was not loony at all, but I suspect the smile on my face must have appeared that I thought so.

I quickly learned Bill wanted to hang out, attend Padres games, my favorite, meet my family, and show me what he did professionally. When it came time for selecting a major for Notre Dame, he said I could bounce ideas off him. This truly helped because not only did I receive solid advice from a prosperous businessman (so what if he attended rival Purdue University, leading me to call him "Boiler"

Bill?), I saw his commitment to helping youth. It instilled in me, before I ever attended my first day of college, these ideals: you must think big to achieve big; dreams do come true; and what value is success unless you can pass it on to others?

Bill was there on the day Attorney Clifford Imbro contacted me after reading the *Union-Tribune* article as well and offered his service pro bono. Dapperly, Imbro suggested since my visa had expired, the best thing to do was appear before an immigration judge.

The judge would rule whether I deserved permanent legal residence, which after five years would make me eligible for U.S. citizenship, or another fate: deportation back to Colombia.

In the meantime, what was I to do about Notre Dame? Immigration cases can take up to a year just to be scheduled, and I was expected at Notre Dame that fall.

A preliminary hearing was set for the judge to schedule a date and Imbro reminded me it might be close to the holidays. This would further delay the proceeding.

He was right. It was near a holiday, but a summer one, the Fourth of July. This was only six weeks away. Depending how the judged ruled I could potentially celebrate a picnic and fireworks in the U.S. or be returned to Colombia.

Earlier in the spring a gentleman named Bob Mundy from Notre Dame's Admissions Office called to let me know my application had been received. I informed him of my pending immigration case and Bob was concerned. He kept in close contact and feared that even just scheduling a suspended deportation case may take so long it might prevent me from enrolling in the fall or for a month-long summer orientation program.

That July morning the skies were atypical steel gray. My Mom's mood matched the weather and she asked in the car, "Are you nervous?"

"No." I lied. I was nervous. I could not afford for God to fail me now.

Driving to the downtown San Diego courthouse, I glanced down at my mother's black leather bag.

Inside were two airline tickets. By that evening, I would either unpack my bag in a strange bedroom in Colombia or in a dorm.

As we arrived to the courthouse, a phalanx of TV cameras greeted us. I hadn't anticipated there would be so much interest. Supporters packed the courtroom—among them Boiler Bill, Mrs. Whitmore, Dr. Amparan, Margarita, and countless friends.

The judge stepped up to his bench. In a brisk manner, he asked for the portfolio containing my academic certificates and letters of recommendation.

Imbro, again impeccably dressed and contained,

started the proceedings by telling the judge how I came to the U.S. and why my visa expired.

The judge then turned to me and rolling up the sleeves of his black robe intoned, "Young man, although you have accomplished much in your eighteen years, I still need to know why I should let you stay, and if I don't, how will you feel?"

I felt my heart pounding through my perspired wet shirt.

"Um, Your Honor," I began. "I love the United States. This country has always given me the only thing I ever asked for—opportunity. I don't remember much about Colombia because I moved away when I was so young, but I know there wasn't much opportunity there for disabled people." I continued. "I've grown up here and I want to grow old here. I want to go to Notre Dame, start a good career, and contribute to this nation. If I don't get to do all that, I'm still blessed just to have spent time here." I looked past his face at the American flag. "This is the greatest country in the world and I'll always be thankful for my time in the United States."

I meant it with all my heart. This country with all its prospect, these citizens who collectively supported me, encouraged me, took me under their wings, one couldn't ask for more. And I would accept my fate.

"You overcame many obstacles," the judge looked

at my hooks. "And surely you will have many more to come. But this is the greatest country in the world and you clearly recognize that." He closed the book in front of him, smiled at me and said, "I am granting you permanent legal residence, Mr. Montoya. Welcome to your future in America."

My heart soared once I caught my breath.

The next day's front page of the *Union-Tribune* called it the fastest immigration case on record.

Mama allowed me to soak in the hugs and limelight, and then reminded me she needed to get me to the airport. The skies cleared up on the short drive to the airport and on the way, Mama pulled out two tickets, ripping one and handing me the other.

Bill handed me a clunker of a device called a car phone. I had learned the airport in South Bend was used by both Indiana and Michigan so they combined the name. I then dialed Bob Mundy's number. "Hello, Bob? Think you can swing by the Michiana Airport around 10pm?"

CHANGE, CHANGE AT OL' NOTRE DAME

I had never previously visited, but had heard and read plenty about the University of Notre Dame. It was reputedly a marvelous place to matriculate, resplendent with colossal school spirit, soaring fall colors, and a closeness among the student body inherent in its population size—10,000—and emphasis on spirituality. Before long I saw it was everything I'd dreamed and more. The glistening Golden Dome, lush green ivy on the sturdy brick facades and overwhelming fervor of football weekends each aroused the soul. Church bells rang hourly, crosses were in every classroom, and each dormitory had a small chapel for weekly worship. It felt like a Norman Rockwell painting with a spiritual emphasis. This was always my top choice and now it was my top example of a dream fulfilled.

It all started with Bob Mundy picking me up at the airport. Meeting him face-to-face he immediately struck me as an Alan Alda look-alike. He sounded like Alda too. He was a realist and blended old-fashion work ethic with enough leeway for dreams to still grow. "Alejandro," he said, "Notre Dame is what you make of it. Whatever you get out of it is whatever you first put in."

This leads me to my next principle:

Leave Every Place Better Than When You Got There

Within days, it became apparent Bob would be my newest mentor, my first one outside of San Diego. He provided sage advice in selecting classes, clothes for the upcoming fall and winter, and how to navigate through the large and daunting campus. Bob wanted me to be active, join organizations, attend lectures and speeches, and become involved in community service. Of course, I had to get good grades first. As my first semester developed, I had an amazing time getting involved with a myriad of activities. There were so many things to partake and naturally, every freshman feels the exuberance of newfound freedom as well. However, there was one aspect that was limiting my unabashed liberty.

What made campus especially tricky was it was old. Notre Dame was over 150 years old and though I loved the story of the French priest Edward Sorin founding the University through rugged individualism, envisioning a world-renowned Catholic institution, enduring multiple fires destroying the original Golden Dome, it was still old. And old meant inaccessible for students with disabilities.

That year, 1992, Congress and the president signed into law the landmark Americans with Disabilities Act (ADA). This was essentially a civil rights law for the disabled community mandating buildings, sidewalks, schools, offices, everywhere to be as accessible as possible.

To me the invisible injustice was present in Notre Dame's most important edifice: the Main Administration Building, which sat beneath the famous Golden Dome. This building had four floors, including the president's office and in my first semester, I was in a weekly Literature class taught by the president. I soon learned that in order to reach Father Edward Malloy's class, I'd have to traverse four flights of stairs. The Administration Building had no elevator.

It was a weekly class gathered each Sunday evening and throughout my four years remained my all-time favorite. That notwithstanding, it was an obstacle to go to class. The stairs were old and creaky and on days where I was wearing snow boots and carrying a heavy book bag, a two-minute jaunt up was transformed into a ten-minute journey of sweat and deep breathing. It just didn't seem fair. And what would happen if a student in a wheelchair someday had this class?

President Malloy—who went by the nickname "Monk"—was sensitive to my needs, but said installing an elevator would require a complete renovation of the building. "I'm sorry, Alex, but the class is going to stay in this building. I will ask the other students if they can help you in carrying your book bag. But for now that's all we can do."

Monk was a tremendous teacher, eloquent with a colossal love of books and knowledge of cultural diversity. However, on the issue of accessibility, I told him he was being shortsighted. "Monk, it is not easy climbing stairs with one prosthetic leg, especially on days I have to wear snow boots. I'll find a way, though. But what if one of your students is in a wheelchair? What are you going to do then?"

He had no answer. And I wondered what was I going to do.

I went to complain to Bob, whose office was fortunately on the first floor of the Main Administration Building. "Ale-HAN-dro, you can do more than just complain about the elevator," he said. "You can make people see all the changes we need to implement here. You'll be gone in four years, but you can impact change for future students. That's how it should be every place you go; you should leave it better than it was when you arrived.

I knew I'd have to find a way to work within the system to impact change. As the ADA would open doors—literally—for students with disabilities, more of them would be looking for high-caliber institutions and I wanted them to have the option of selecting Notre Dame.

I embarked on a massive campaign of writing letters, penning opinion pieces for the school newspaper, *The Observer*—ah—the power of writing again! I contacted administration and student leaders via the fabulous new technology called email. What I emphasized in proclaiming the need for accessibility was even those who weren't disabled probably knew someone that was—and not to be grim, but any able-bodied person can become disabled tomorrow. Accessibility, I argued, affected us all.

I never picketed. I never protested. Not that I disagree with those forms of democratic expressions. Working within the system, in this case, I believed was the smartest method.

Near the end of my freshman year, after the snow melted and thunderstorms crackled as a sign of pending spring, Monk called my dorm room. The distance between his office and my cherished St. Edward's Hall was only a few feet, but I dreaded each step. Maybe I had gone too far, maybe pushed the envelope a little too much this time, which Monk once accurately noted I liked to do and now risked the wrath of his anger.

After trudging the four flights of stairs, Monk greeted me and allowed me to catch my breath. "Alex, what do you hope to see by the time you graduate from Notre Dame?"

"A national championship in football and," I took a deep breath, "an elevator in this building."

He chuckled. "Well, I can't promise you a championship, although a better defense would help. But I can promise you..."

Monk then picked up a binder from his desk, cradling it in his large fingers that belied his former days as a Notre Dame basketball player. "This," he said with a slight smile, "is a report on what we're going to do on campus relative to access changes. You may not be here to see this, but this entire Administration Building will be renovated—which means we will have an elevator."

"Awesome! I mean, uh, very well...sir."

"Overseeing this will be the Office for Students with Disabilities."

I was confused. "But sir, we don't have an Office for Students with Disabilities."

"We do now. It will open in 1995 on the South Quad."

I was too stunned and giddy to hear him ask, "So do you agree, all we need is a better defense to win a championship, right?" His grin matched mine, though my expression far more dazed.

Soon renovations were done to several, ancient buildings. Monk pushed the Board of Trustees and the Main Building, needing of a facelift anyhow, underwent a multi-million dollar overhaul—including new elevators.

Previously disability issues were handled by a campus-wide volunteer committee comprised of administrators from varying departments, including Bob. It was disbanded and Notre Dame joined its peers by opening a full-time Disability Services Center—for students and faculty—and Bob helped choose its new director. I was honored in October 1995, when, in my senior year, Fr. Malloy blessed the new center and asked me to speak at its grand opening.

I knew I would be gone by 1996. This in pushing for a permanent disability services program, others—with far greater expertise and pedigree—could look after these issues long after I graduated. I made an impact on an institution others could enjoy. I left the place better than I found it. I say it with all humility and gratitude.

May we all have that opportunity once in our lives. Leave a place better than you found it and make a mark, lasting forever.

WINNING WITH LOU HOLTZ

When I was at Notre Dame, I made it a goal to meet the head football coach of the Fighting Irish, Lou Holtz. Not only had he won a national championship for the school in 1988, but Holtz authored several motivational books and was as passionate about being a champion in life as much as he was in athletics. He demonstrated such skill in motivating and captivating others that corporations paid up to $15,000 to have him deliver keynote addresses.

I barely had $15, let alone $15,000, as a college sophomore but in the summer of '93, I was determined to gain an audience with Sweet Lou. Thus, I displayed the type of tenacity and persistence I continued to use later in pursuing a potential employer—that is, I allowed myself to cross the line and become a nuisance.

After sending Holtz a letter introducing myself and simply saying I wanted 20 minutes of his time to learn more about his views on accomplishments,

I pestered his secretary with follow-up calls. Not to the point where any restraining orders were issued, but close. I knew too, summer school was his most flexible time of the year—no games, practices, or recruiting trips—that I subtly reminded him of through my messages to his assistant.

For me this wasn't just a starry-eyed attempt to meet a celebrity and have him autograph my napkin from the dining hall; I truly wanted to forsake the usual banter about zone defenses and beating Michigan and hone in on talking about persistence and success. What was it that allowed Holtz to inherit five losing college football teams, including Notre Dame, and have them in bowl games by his second season at each place? Why was he as passionate about writing and talking about overcoming adversity as he was about beating the stuffing out of USC?

Being a believer you put yourself in position to succeed and sometimes opportunity will knock unexpectedly, and it did. Finally after weeks of dogged persistence, Holtz's secretary left me a voicemail saying her boss agreed to meet me. The time frame was even shorter than I had requested, 15 minutes, and it had to be the next day or never.

I already knew the primary questions I would ask Holtz based on the book, *Winning Every Day,* he wrote following ND's championship season five years earlier: a book that not only navigated his team's conquests, but the personal truths he lived by as well. Bob Mundy loaned me that masterpiece, which I tucked away in my belongings hoping he would forget I had it.

I must confess the time Holtz set for our rendez-vous conflicted with one of my classes and not only did I spurn Chemistry 101 for Holtz 101, but I also convinced a pal to do the same.

"Ian Hernández, what will you remember most when you graduate and return to Houston," I asked him, "decoding DNA or sitting on Lou Holtz's leather couch?" Sure enough, Ian succumbed to my reasoning. We then met the man whose office had also been occupied by gridiron legends like Knute Rockne, Frank Leahy, and Ara Parseghian.

Holtz stood about 5'10" but was not more than 150 pounds soaking wet and looked almost diminutive in his pale blue sweater and khaki pants. It was hard to tell which overshadowed his tan face, the oversized wire-rim glasses or his mussed sandy-blonde hair.

He spoke with a lisp and noticed right away I looked different than most that reached out to shake his hand. He reached and greeted me with, "Shun, I've never shaken a hook before. How do you move those things?"

I explained how whenever I moved a shoulder, the strap harness that connected my arms across my back would pull the proper cable to move my hook or elbow joint. If I wanted to move my elbow up or down it required a shoulder movement in a different direction. Since I was wearing some typically garish 1990s neon-green shorts, I observed Holtz scanning my leg. So I described my hip was fused when I was too young to remember and the prosthetic I wore contained a knee joint with a spring which allowed me to walk and run.

This launched a summary, at his request, of my views on overcoming adversity, maintaining a positive attitude, and never yielding to the temptation to give up. Holtz particularly liked it when I quoted from the book *Grit, Guts, & Genius*—a compilation of motivational figures including him: "Ability is what you're capable of doing. Motivation determines what you do. Attitude determines how well you do it."

However, Holtz was not completely satisfied.

"Shun, I admire you, but you're forgetting one key component," said the 55-year-old coach as he pulled up a chair next to wide-eyed Ian and me. "There's more to life than just overcoming challenges. You do that out of necessity. I want you to learn how to live a life of excellence and how to *win*."

As he fixed a steely glare on us, Sweet Lou uncoiled a passionate sermon on how the people he most admired were overachievers. He was one himself. Coming from a modest family in West Virginia, he had neither wealth nor great athletic skill, yet trained himself to learn every position on his high school football team. In that manner he could be inserted anywhere if a front-line starter needed rest or became injured. He finished 234th academically in a high school class of 278, yet was persistent in becoming a college football coach. His primary dream though was to be the head football coach at Notre Dame and he held on to that goal with such conviction that whatever losing program he was reviving had to agree to insert a contractual clause allowing him to apply for the Fighting Irish job if one ever opened.

In late 1985, it became available. Holtz left another improbable success story at the University of Minnesota to take over Notre Dame's historic yet flagging program. The first thing he did was raise the standards whereby if star players were even late for team meetings, they didn't play. If stringent academic standards were not met, they did not play. If a prized recruit did not demonstrate as much interest in receiving an education as much as he did playing in Notre Dame Stadium, Holtz canceled his visit to the recruit's home.

"Shun, I raised the standards and you must do the shame!" I recognized by now, "shame" meant "same" and Holtz's intense inflection meant business.

He continued, "You've achieved a lot already, but I won't truly be impressed unless you overachieve. Raise the bar. Do *more* than what is expected of you."

What Holtz meant by telling us he wanted to see us win had nothing to do with scoreboard results. *WIN* was an acronym for:

What's Important Now

What Holtz was demanding was that I take it a step further and raise my expectations regarding grades, campus activities, and personal goals.

In each instance when it came time to focus on time management, he said a champion narrows his focus to doing What's Important Now. When you get bombarded with requests for your time, simply ask What's Important Now. In listing 100 things you want to accomplish in your life—which Holtz did in 1966, actually listing 107 and thus far achieving over half of them—think about What's Important Now.

"In times of crisis," he continued, "you can be the calmest person in the room if, while everyone is going berserk, you focus on What's Important Now and take it step by step. Same thing with personal adversity—if you get down you shouldn't be down for long if you think about What's Important Now and go from there."

I saw why football players a foot taller and invariably thicker—standouts who eventually played professionally like Tim Brown, Raghib "Rocket" Ismael, Jerome Bettis, and John Carney listened intently to this man who was so small many dubbed him Leprechaun Lou. Or why corporations like IBM and 3M paid thousands for speeches in a pronounced lisp and a straightforward vocabulary.

He kept it simple but passionate. Holtz had no use for people, be they athletes or audience members, who pitied themselves or maintained a low standard for life goals. In his mind overachievers were really misnomers because we all should strive to overachieve.

When Lou Holtz used words like "excellence" and "persistence," spittle flew out of his mouth and into our laps. But, Ian and I ignored that and focused on the meaning behind his fiery (and wet) words.

It wasn't pie-in-the-sky stuff either. All adversity can be overcome if you think about What's Important Now in regard to goals, dreams, time management, even relationships.

Lou Holtz's final words were, "Shun, I want you to keep in touch and tell me how you exceeded expectations set by yourself and others. I'm glad you don't allow others to feel sorry for you. Now go out and do more than that. Don't just live a life of overcoming, but of *excellence*."

We maintained correspondence through my

graduation in the spring of '96 and that fall Holtz felt his time at Notre Dame was complete, opting to resurrect another moribund program at the University of South Carolina. On that steamy summer afternoon in South Bend he lit a new fire under me. We were supposed to talk for 15 minutes. Ian and I left his office an hour later.

Long after I left Notre Dame, I incorporated the *What's Important Now* mantra in choosing how to use my time, how to foster any relationships and how to accomplish long-term goals by establishing smaller and more immediate ones.

CARRYING THE TORCH

The greatest honor that I received thus far in my life was announced to me on a miserable, soggy late-spring afternoon in Indiana. If you are inclined to find metaphors or comparisons between weather patterns and life emotions, this day was suited for that. It was the final semester of my senior year and all my struggles were becoming crystallized for me. Feeling conflicted—sad to soon be leaving Notre Dame, yet eager for another long winter to end—I headed to my dorm in St. Edward's Hall. I snuck a peek at the statue of Mary atop the Golden Dome and wondered, *Can I make it through my last semester? And if I do, was it worth it? I have no job lined up, have no plans, have no...*

To match my mood, the slow thaw of winter melted into a constant flood of rain. Gray skies formed into an unchanging backdrop and out of 30 days in April of 1996, 26 of them were rainy. Sad but true. South Bend was never going to be compared with San Diego, but I didn't expect it to be like Seattle either!

As I was sinking into a pity party, I arrived at my dorm room and pulled out a small garage door opener. As part of their newfound commitment to accessibility, the university wired my door so instead of fumbling with lock and key, all I had to do was press a button on my opener. My roommates John and Victor loved it because it impressed the girls. The only logical thing was to retreat and take a nap. We don't give naps their just due in refreshing the mind and body. They worked in kindergarten and most definitely in college—as well as European and South American countries under the auspices of *siestas*—so why do we not have naps in the workplace? But I digress.

Just as I entered into that sweet moment when consciousness faded into a dream state, I heard noises. And the next thing I knew my body was being shaken. "Wake up! Wake up!" It was Victor. How dare he! I was especially mad, because I let him play his San Antonio Tex-Mex music as loud as he wanted even when I needed some peace and quiet. So, when he roused me, I grabbed one of the boots he used for Mexican *Folklorico* dancing and flung it at him.

John quickly came to his defense. Raising his voice with the firmness he learned growing up in

Brooklyn, "If you'll wake up and stop complaining, we actually got good news for your sleepy ass!"

A member of the Fighting Irish fencing team, I didn't mess with John, because that may result in a saber to the chest. So I relented. I sat up, noticed the day-old Papa John's Pizza—a Midwest necessity—and grabbed a slice to reawaken my senses.

They handed me a large white envelope, which I saw was already open.

"We already read it," chuckled Vic, "now you need to read it, Paco!"

Paco was what my friends called me as a humorous reference to an airline attendant in Tennessee who once called me Mr. "Montaco." Thus Paco provided a nice rhyme to it.

The envelope had both an insignia from the United Way and Olympic Host Committee. I unfolded the letter but before I got past "Dear Alex Montoya..."

John blurted out, "You're going to—"

Just then the phone rang. "Hold on." I said reaching for the telephone.

"Alejandro?"

It was Bob Mundy.

"Yes, Bob," I waved my roommates to sit down and shut up.

"Alejandro, have you read your mail yet?"

"I was just getting to it."

"Let me save you some work, young lad. I just got cc'd on a letter you received today."

Uh-oh. Were my grades not good enough to earn my diploma? Did I skip too many early morning classes? Darn that eight o'clock Civil War class taught by wide-eyed Father Kirby!

By this time, John and Victor were beside themselves.

"You are going to carry the Olympic torch!" John screamed.

I was dumbfounded! I glanced over the letter. Sure enough that is what it said. Forgetting I was holding the slice of pizza and the telephone, I jumped up and down causing pieces of pepperoni to land on Victor's dancing boots.

"Alejandro, Alejandro!" Bob was shouting over the dangling phone line.

I picked up the handset, "Yes, yes, I am sorry. I think I know what I am reading."

"Alejandro, you are going to do what you have been doing your entire life: carry the torch." He sounded uncommonly giddy.

It took several re-reads of the letter to completely comprehend it. It was true. And then, I ran up and down the hallways of St. Ed's in amazement and glee, leaving Bob hanging on the phone again.

Apparently, there was a nomination period for people to be one of the 10,000 torchbearers to deliver the flame—once it reached America from its native Athens, Greece—to Atlanta, Georgia, home of that summer's Olympic Games. Torchbearers were sought who overcame adversity and were involved in community service. As it turned out, Shriners' Hospital officials in Los Angeles (where I had transferred to from the San Francisco facility as a teen because of L.A.'s proximity to San Diego) nominated me. I immediately called to thank them, still in disbelief I was nominated and actually chosen.

From then on my final semester had an added sense of importance and delightful glee. Not only did I feel honored to participate, but it wasn't until later that I learned how much more significant it would be to carry this torch.

A couple months later, just two weeks after I'd graduated, Bob loaded up the Mundy Mobile with his family and me—whom he often called "the teenager I never wanted"—and we drove to where I was going to carry the torch.

The location for that majestic day was a small town to the south, near Indianapolis, called Rensselear. Understand when I say a small town, Rensselear (pronounced Ren-sell-ear) made South Bend look like Las Vegas. This was hometown Americana at its best, a Norman Rockwell painting forever set in 1957.

Dressed in a white t-shirt with matching mesh

shorts, both with the Olympic logo adorned across the front, I was instructed to arrive at the front steps of City Hall. This building was just like one you'd see in an old black-and-white movie, with a large stairwell leading up to a concrete door inscribed... well...City Hall.

It was nearly noon on yet another drizzly and bleak cloud-covered day when the ultra-caffeinated event coordinator—Mindy, or Cindy, or Katie I think it was—excitedly said, "The whole town will be here to watch you, Mr. Montaya!" (I get no respect.)

And Mr. Montaya wasn't lied to. I'm not sure of the approximate population of Renssalear, Indiana, but if it was 3,000 people then 3,000 of them showed up at City Hall. There with an endless sea of cameras, star-spangled hats, and American flags.

Speaking of flags, each torchbearer—there were three of us that day and I was kicking off the procession at City Hall—was given a large purple flag on a thin wooden pole. We were to choose someone to take this flag and meet us about a half-mile from where our point in the relay began, at which point we'd greet the next Olympic torch bearer. Mindy/Cindy said the purple flag would be a noticeable landmark, and whoever held it should be a person we both trusted and cared for. I chose Bob Mundy.

After a brief ceremony in which several local and state politicians spoke, the procession began. It was mind-boggling to me that before my very eyes was the Olympic Flame, the same one lit in Greece, protected every night in a cauldron which ensured it never went out, traveled cross-country by horseback, trains, and motorcades until it reached Indiana. This same flame would last all the way until weeks later, when gorgeous swimmer Janet Evans would take her torch, Muhammad Ali his and overcoming the shakiness of his Parkinson's Disease would light the massive torch above the opening ceremonies.

There is a wide misconception the torch relay is one torch being passed from person to person. It is not. There are actually 10,000 torches, each made with a smooth wooden handle and metallic top and each torchbearer gets his/her flame from the person before them. They run or walk—I mostly walked—the estimated half-mile. Then one lowers the tip of their torch lighting the next person's torch. It is a true relay, much like runners passing a baton.

The torch itself was heavy. It was twenty pounds of gilded silver, gold, and wood base. I could feel the heat from the flame on my face.

As I carried my torch a volunteer pre-selected from the community assisted me in clutching it; as we walked we had the torch directly between us. Even this strapping young man talked about how honored he felt to be a participant.

With four police officers on motorcycles in front

of me and a Secret Service—whoa!—agent behind, there was an air of importance and drama. But before I even had time to feel cocky, I scanned the crowd and was amazed by what I saw.

Every person roped off to either side had either a still or video camera. Necks were craned and American flags of all sizes waved deliriously. There was even a murmur among the crowd, which rose to a crescendo as the torch came closer to them. That was followed by applause and even gasps as the torch passed by.

But then I realized something disturbing. The gasps were not all directed toward the specter of seeing the Olympic torch. Some of the gasps were directed toward me.

With my shorts and t-shirt, they could clearly see my three prosthetics, which led to numerous looks of astonishment. Many nudged and whispered to each other. A few mothers hid their children's eyes. Suddenly my immense pride withered into feeling awkward, even grotesque.

Back home in San Diego, Mama wouldn't like how I allowed the town folk to make me feel that way, but those were my immediate emotions. Suffering, I continued to walk.

Then about halfway through the route, I caught a glimmer of shiny metal from the corner of my eye. It was a man sitting in a wheelchair and when

I turned my head to see him, I noticed him sitting beside five other men in wheelchairs.

Each of them was bearded and wearing baseball caps, a couple of them donning green military jackets. Behind them was an entire row of older men, which based on their white hair and smaller hats, I deduced to be a veteran's group. With a quick nod of my head, I indicated to my walking partner to shift to the right so the veterans could see the torch up close.

As we approached the rope, their eyes lit up. I saw many of these men were missing legs, or arms, and used either wheelchairs or canes. Their apparel confirmed that they were indeed veterans, as evidenced by words scrawled across their jackets and hats like Korea, Vietnam, and Persian Gulf.

They gazed at the torch, now mere inches from them, and those who weren't touching it, were taking pictures. More than one had tears in his eyes.

As I pulled away a few minutes later, one of them made a thumbs-up gesture, wiped his eyes dry, and mouthed out to me, "Thank...you."

Precisely at that moment, I no longer felt like the freak.

What I realized was these gentlemen related to me. Perhaps they endured an even stronger sense of scorn when they returned to town, especially if the war was unpopular.

But I felt just as connected with them. It occurred to me I wouldn't even be here, living in freedom, had it not been for the heroism of these former soldiers. Heroism is the exact word; as much as I love sports, I detest it when an announcer calls an athlete "heroic" just because they hit the game-winning home run or basket. Athletes are incredible entertainers and role models but not, by definition, heroes. Men and women who fight to protect our freedom are heroes.

Those veterans fought to protect the American way of life, just as veterans before them had done the same. As they grew older, they were passing the torch to the next generation to continue working toward improving the USA in any way possible. Their sacrifices made it possible for me to live in a country of endless opportunity.

As I reached the end of my run and finally saw Bob Mundy, he came up to me.

"You carried the torch today, Alejandro, for all those who overcome adversity, for your family in Colombia, and for the future generations to come. That's what life is all about, my lad. Someone carried the torch of opportunity before you and you will do the same for future Latinos and disabled kids. This torch is made of metal, but the torch you carry cannot be seen—but it sure can be felt."

It is my responsibility then to carry that torch to

those younger than me, providing tomorrow's leaders with knowledge, motivation, and opportunity. Every person who went before me—veterans, activists, even my parents (both sets)—opened doors for me to walk through. I realized I must do the same, just as you must.

We have a responsibility to improve our society for the future generations. That is the torch we each carry. Just like the Olympic torch was protected day and night, our personal torch must never go out. Never let that flame of inspiration or hope extinguish.

We are all torchbearers. We are all part of what I call the Torch Relay of Life. Living an extraordinary life is my torch I pass to you.

You can make a difference.

ROOKIE BALL

After the Torch Run, I bid a sad farewell to Indiana and returned to the paradise of San Diego. With zero job prospects yet teeming with confidence and hope, I decided before I left South Bend to be proactive in my pursuits.

I always had a passion for baseball and because I couldn't swing a bat or catch a ball, I looked for other ways to be involved in the sensational sport. Working for a sports team was another dream and, in particular, the San Diego Padres. They were my team, having earned my loyalty—and fascination— with their gritty, improbable run to the World Series in 1984 when I was ten. They kept my loyalty because through the years the team struggled as a "little guy" in a rapidly growing sport where only bullies—large-market teams—seemed to have a reasonable shot at winning. Yet the Padres persevered and even in the leanest years always maintained their commitment to being extremely generous in the community. I related to their underdog role and was drawn to their civic responsiveness.

The Padres, like all of Major League Baseball, survived a harrowing period in the early 1990s when the national recession and players' strike threatened the sport's very existence. By 1996, the year I graduated from Notre Dame, the team's new owners, John Moores and Larry Lucchino, breathed new life into the franchise. The charismatic Lucchino also resuscitated a moribund Baltimore Orioles organization, and Moores brought him to California to do the same in San Diego.

The many articles written on the Ivy League-educated Lucchino laid out his premise for earning the fans' respect and trust, which he called "organizational pillars": 1. Field a team worthy of the fans' affection. 2. Improve the game day atmosphere into a more entertaining one. 3. Be even more active in the community, while marketing the team to a broader audience in the region.

This last point really caught my eye because, for all their great deeds, the Padres had historically not done much outreach to San Diego's urban neighborhoods or marketed to Mexico—which was just a twenty-minute drive south to the border.

With swiftness and aggressiveness—and really with nothing to lose—I wrote a letter to Lucchino asking for a job in his promising organization. I anticipated that Lucchino as president and CEO would eventually get around to receiving and reading it, and I might—*might*—get a response after a month.

He wrote back in one week.

Thus on a muggy afternoon suitable for shorts and flip-flops, I was happy to don a heavy black jacket, slacks, shirt, and tie. Lucchino emphasized in his response letter that nothing was promised, but I'd be granted a series of job interviews with some of his top executives (he was unfortunately out of town that day).

There may be nothing more nerve-racking than a job interview. I hoped this dream came true.

I met with Lucchino's Directors of Human Resources, Marketing, and Community Relations. Each was genuinely nice, and I could immediately see the Padres would succeed in their post-strike campaign slogan: "*The New Padres: We Want You Back!*"

I thought, *I didn't necessarily want to be back, I just wanted them to want me!*

After reviewing my résumé and asking a series of questions aimed to learn more about my experiences and future visions, I heard some fairly underwhelming responses:

"You're a great kid."

Oh, good they like me.

"I sure wish my department had an opening right now, we could use you."

Wait. No. No. No!

"Someday you will surely be a success."

Someday?

The most straightforward response I received was from Michele Anderson, who headed up the Community Relations wing.

"Alex, you have a great history, but unfortunately not a professionally related one. You're not sure what it is you want to do. My advice is to go out and get some experience, build up your résumé, and keep in touch with me along the way. I fully expect to see you back here someday."

As I left Jack Murphy Stadium, where the team's offices were located, those words were well intentioned but the turndown still stung. Walking away, I felt my limp more pronounced. Just as with Notre Dame, this was where I wanted to be and this was what I wanted to do.

But then, I realized Michele was right. I had no jobs outside of part-time college ones, no strong community contacts in a professional sense, and truly had no idea what to do with my Communications degree.

Just as the Padres were a major league team, I had to fight my way through the minor leagues to earn the right to be with them. Michele's forthright advice was exactly what I needed.

I commenced to fire off a series of résumés and cover letters to every public relations and marketing company in San Diego County. If they didn't have job openings, I was willing to take an internship (although I'd had one in the sports department of the NBC affiliate in South Bend). If they didn't have an internship, I was willing to take fifteen minutes of advice if they would sit and dispense it to me.

Surely, a Communications degree from the University of Notre Dame, coupled with a sturdy list of community involvement and a few honors merited an interview, right? Or at least a dialogue. Or at a minimum a courtesy phone call.

I mailed approximately 100 letters.

I received one phone call back.

The voice was gruff and impatient. "Montoya, my name is David Nuffer. I got your letter and I guess we can meet, hell, why not."

Taken aback he referred to me solely by my last name and since there weren't any other opportunities pending, I took him up on his offer.

"Um, thank you, Mr. Nuffer," I replied, "can we meet…"

"Aw crap, don't call me Mister, makes me feel old! Call me Dave. I'm free all day on Friday and my office is in Mission Hills, just north of downtown. Come when you like. Byeeee."

He stretched out the "bye" as I stretched out my hopes, truly yearning for this chat to lead to employment.

I scheduled my visit to Nuffer, Smith, Tucker (NST) Communications for early afternoon on the following Friday so I could be home in time to watch that evening's Padres game. The Friars—the team's secondary nickname because of the religious friar moniker had been buried but resurrected by Lucchino—were embroiled in a late-season pennant race with the Los Angeles Dodgers, and missing a game was like missing one's favorite *novela,* or soap opera.

Remembering Mr. Nuffer, er, Dave's intimidating phone etiquette, I entered his office cautiously.

Rapping lightly on his half-open door, I heard, "Yeah, come in."

But as I stepped in, I didn't see anyone.

"Mr. Nuffer? Dave?"

Then I saw him. On the ground, sliding piles of paper under his desk as a makeshift filing system.

He rose and grinned. His cheeks quite rosy and his thick eyebrows matching his stark-white mane. "So, you must be Montoya."

Nuffer, although Caucasian, emphasized the Spanish pronunciation of my surname. *Moan-Toy-a.*

As I nervously slid into a chair, my eyes darted

across his office. Nuffer had books and pictures of Hemingway, bullfighters, Aztec art, and...oh...

"I see you have an autographed baseball?" I half-asked, half-stated.

"Yes," Nuffer replied, his eyes twinkling. "You like baseball?"

My confidence surged. "Absolutely."

Nuffer leaned forward and stared. "Who's your team?"

"The Padres!"

"Good," easing back into his chair. "I thought maybe you were going to say the Dodgers. I hate the Dodgers!"

This led to a lengthy conversation about his Steve Garvey baseball, signed in 1983 and rightfully predicting a World Series berth in '84, and heaps of baseball trivia and storytelling. Along the way we got to my résumé and career ambitions.

"Montoya, I remember those stories they did on you about the deportation case," he said. "I like you, not just because you think we'll win the pennant, but because of who you are. You deserve a chance to succeed. So I'm going to break a longstanding rule of mine and let you—a non-San Diego State student—apply for our paid internship."

"Thank you, Mr. Nu-, uh, Dave!"

"Now I haven't promised you anything," Dave retorted standing and clutching a baseball mitt, "but come back next Friday and I'll have you meet my staff and take a writing test. If you're any good, maybe we'll hire you."

I stood up, thanked him again, and prepared to exit before he changed his mind.

"Montoya," I heard. Oh, no. I looked back.

"Very nice to meet you, *compadre*."

On the last weekend of September 1996, the Padres swept Los Angeles in a three-game series, clinching the National League West pennant on a sun-splashed and exhilarating afternoon at Dodger Stadium. It was the team's first playoff appearance since magical 1984.

The day after my team sealed the triumph, I started my first day as an NST Communications intern.

Back then, we used pagers, which seem superfluous now, but in the mid-90s pagers were how people reached you before everyone owned cell phones. My mentors, Kuni, Mundy and now Nuffer kept my pager humming.

One of the client accounts Nuffer had me work with was The Access Center of San Diego, a United Way agency specializing in helping people with disabilities find accessible housing and other independent-living services. After my internship expired, The

Access Center invited me to join their staff full-time and Nuffer gave his blessing.

Still one eye was kept on the Padres and, as Michele advised, I kept her informed of my career path. Each time she sent kind congratulatory notes. I could not, would not, lose my sights on working full-time for the Padres.

In my third year at the Access Center, in 1999, Mark Guglielmo of the Padres contacted me wanting to host a job fair. His goal was to recruit people with disabilities for their event staff, which, of course, made me start thinking.

We joined forces and hosted the job fair. Then I surprised Guglielmo by applying for a part-time ushering position.

"With a degree from Notre Dame and with a full-time job already," he inquired, "why would you want to become an usher?"

Others asked the same question. What they saw was a strictly seasonal game day-only, low-paying blue-collar position. They also cringed when I described I'd have to head to Qualcomm Stadium after a day's work at the Access Center, plus work late into the night, weekends, and holidays.

But what I recognized was *opportunity.* I had to be in it to win it.

A chance to be a part of the thrill of Major League Baseball. A chance to meet the Padres' decision-makers and witness the behind-the-scenes action of putting on games. A step toward making another dream come true.

I applied and interviewed the next day.

They hired me two days later.

Gazing at the field my first day on the job, which was undergoing preparations in February, I knew I'd see it every day come April. I was part of the Padres—even if it was on a part-time basis!

And still I dreamed bigger.

HOORAY FOR HOLLYWOOD

How can I live a successful life? How can I overcome my personal challenges? What are the keys to happiness and fulfillment?

Those are easily the three questions I am asked most frequently.

My next principle:

Focus On What You Have, Not On What You Are Missing

Many people are amazed when they meet me and tell me they are praying for me "to someday have arms or not be disabled." I tell them, and quite frankly often in a testy tone, to pray for my family, future, or well-being. Praying I will someday look physically different is completely unnecessary. That is because, as instilled in me by Mama at an early age, I was too busy enjoying what I had to think about what I was missing.

I never grew up lamenting because I was missing

my arms or right leg. Mama taught me to be excited I could read and write and—often to her chagrin—talk. She taught me instead of feeling frustrated because I couldn't swing a bat like Steve Garvey or shoot a basketball like Michael Jordan (though who can?) to be grateful I could kick a soccer ball. Because of my hooks I couldn't even be a receiver in the neighborhood pick-up football, but I could run fast enough to chase people around and blitz the quarterback full-time. Even though I would've loved to emulate The Garv or Air Jordan, I simply accepted that I didn't have the physical capacity to do so.

I am not bitter about my challenges—because I am too busy enjoying life. I was always immersed in school, sports, and social activities, focusing on what I had instead of what I was missing. Mama told me, "Accept your challenges. Know you have limitations. Then forget about them. Keep your mind on what you have and what you can do. That will keep you living as you should be—doing whatever you want to do."

That's when Stuntman Dave entered my life. Or, to be exact, re-entered it.

Stuntman Dave was David Smith, a tall and bearded chap who was missing one arm due to a childhood accident. He parlayed his disability into a successful stunt man career, convincing casting directors that movies would appear more realistic if someone, say, who had an arm blown off was truly missing an arm. He appeared in a variety of action films in the 1980s and 90s, and was the primary stunt figure for "Terminator II" and "Star Trek V." My high esteem for Dave, and the initial way I got to meet him when I was merely seven, was because he created a group called Stunts-Ability, which held stunt clinics and motivational seminars for amputee children. I really had neither the body size nor the inclination to be a stunt person, but I was enough of a ham—that I was interested in acting. So Dave told me we'd keep in touch—and unlike many in Hollywood he meant it.

In fact for a short period in the early 90s he co-hosted a Southern California cable program highlighting persons with disabilities who were succeeding in life and to my great surprise, he chose me as a guest during my junior year at San Diego High School. (It was that video I sent to Bob Mundy with my admissions packet to Notre Dame.)

Dave contacted me with what I'd assumed was one of his periodic check-ins. But this time he had fantastic news. And puzzling to me. Though he was semi-retired from the stunt industry he still had a bevy of contacts in Los Angeles, one of whom alerted him to an upcoming project. Film director Steven Spielberg was taking on a script left behind by fellow movie giant Stanley Kubrick. The cinematic creation was to be called *AI: Artificial Intelligence,* a futuristic film based on the premise of robots assimilating into human life.

Stuntman Dave told me about how for years Hollywood shunned actors with disabilities because they were viewed as a weak link. They were considered unattractive and pathetic, usually portrayed on screen as either beggars or embittered creatures. He hated those stereotypes and worked fiercely to show the film industry they could use hard workers like him. Now at the dawn of a new century it took no less than the brilliant mind of Steven Spielberg to reverse this way of thinking. If a film was being made which featured characters that were robots, why not make them look as authentic as possible?

I don't know which sounded stranger, the film's plot or Dave taking the time to explain it to me. I didn't even like sci-fi, save for the epic "Star Wars" trilogy or Spielberg's feel-good "E.T." franchise. "And of course, your roles in Star Trek," I explained to Stuntman Dave.

But behind Dave Smith's coarse voice, the kind which sound like swallowed marbles and tonsils smoothed with sandpaper, was an idea. An exciting idea. He rarely wore his hook anymore, finding his one good arm was suitable enough for him, but when he grasped my shoulder it felt like two firm hands shaking me.

As it turns out Spielberg wanted to utilize people who were amputees for the robotic roles. The prosthetics worn by those amputees could be replicated into robotic-looking devices. To get a coveted role one had to audition and Dave knew the people coordinating the tryouts.

"You told me way back when you were seven you would love to be in the movies," Dave said. "Well this is your chance. Even if you never make a career out of it, you can say you gave it a shot. You tried something extraordinary."

My new favorite movie was Tom Cruise's "Jerry Maguire" and just like Jerry is told by Reneé Zellweger, *"You had me at hello,"* Stuntman Dave had me at "extraordinary."

A few weeks later in August 2000 I hopped on a train to downtown Los Angeles, where I caught a taxi to the Studio City part of Tinseltown. Part of me remained detached in that I did not expect this to come to full fruition, yet the other half was wide-eyed and agog by being on a Hollywood lot. A massive mural of the characters on my favorite television show *Friends* greeted me on the Warner Brothers lot and I strolled mesmerized past background sets used for *Bonanza* and *The Munsters*.

In the center of the lot, with golf carts carrying

executives wearing heavy suits in spite of the heat was a set of offices hidden among bungalows. It was there I met up with Stuntman Dave, who had arrived earlier for his scheduled audition.

My audition was nearly a mid-afternoon disaster. So rushed was the process that the casting director handed each aspiring applicant, about twenty of us in total, one piece of paper with three to four typed lines on it. Even my high school and college play auditions taught me you were generally handed a full script and told to read a number of lines often spanning several pages.

Under cloaked secrecy Spielberg instructed his assistants not to divulge the name of any characters or scene details; we received only sparse information. I was told to read one line pretending to be a farmer. In my best countrified accent I blurted out something about a tornado hitting my ranch, realizing there was nothing in my background as a Colombian or Californian that lent any believability to that tone.

One of the casting directors, appearing sympathetic to my obvious nervousness, peered out from behind the tripod they were using to record each audition. She asked if I wanted to read for the role of the doctor. She didn't look up at me.

I raised one eyebrow, smirked and responded,

"Well sure, but I'm not really a doctor. I only play one on TV."

The room remained silent. The casting director finally did look up, but said nothing. I read my ultra-serious doctor's line. "Thank you for your time. We'll be in touch," was all she said.

I was sure I blew it, but two weeks later I was contacted to submit a videotape. Spielberg was making his final decision. Why the king of Hollywood, who had worked with the likes of Harrison Ford, Gwyneth Paltrow, and Drew Barrymore, would need two tapes to decide on hiring a no name like me was baffling. But sure enough a short time later those same casting directors phoned me to say they liked my live audition and taped monologue. Her words of congratulations consisted of: "I'm spending time in Manhattan right now, but just *had* to call you. We think you're funny and have good *sass*. You're a lamb, you *are*."

With that, I was invited to become one of the dozen or so robots appearing in AI. I was told I wouldn't have any lines but my character—and Stuntman Dave's!—would have a specific role and we'd be needed on location in Long Beach for several weeks.

Naturally, I was thrilled. Yet unsure of whether I should take advantage of this opportunity. Would I embarrass myself in front of those other actors, many of whom had roles ranging in films from *Forrest Gump* to *The Perfect Storm?*

Leave it to Mama to provide the definitive answer on those doubts: "You must be crazy if you pass this up. You have dreamed about this your entire life. Now you can do something extraordinary. All your life people have looked at your arms and questioned you or turned from you. Now they *want you* because of your arms and your abilities. This is your chance to make a conscious decision to live out a dream. You have the opportunity, now you need to make it a reality."

Mama was right—when wasn't she? We each have opportunities to choose. Living a dream is also a choice, and it is rooted in initial desire to achieve extraordinary heights according to one's own set of values and goals.

Before I left, Mama bought me a camera to sneak some snapshots of actors I'd come across. Stuntman Dave loaded my duffel bags into his truck—joking I should be easy to transport due to my detachable parts—and we drove from sunny San Diego to hazy Long Beach. There to greet us, in the wee hours of pre-dawn, was a salt-and-pepper bearded man with a wrinkled Yankees cap and faded leather jacket. "Hi, I'm Steven Spielberg."

When it came to the actors who were assembled (not a robot joke, I swear, no pun intended) for this multi-million dollar film, I was clearly on the low end of the totem pole. You had the legendary Spielberg, of course, directing the film and enlisting the help of other top-flight Tinseltown producers, special effects whizzes, and crewmembers. The most prominent actors were promising thespians Jude Law, whose British chops were acclaimed in "Talented Mr. Ripley" and Haley Joel Osment, child actor of "Sixth Sense" fame.

Stopping by for cameos, some of them as voice-overs for the robots, were luminaries like Robin Williams and Chris Rock. Even the guy that formerly was the voice for Smoky the Bear had a role, which I thought was ultra-cool. In stark contrast, there was Alex Montoya, of no fame or credentials, playing a robotic cook who had neither a formal name nor any lines to utter. Although scheduled to be in several scenes, I served mostly as a background player.

So how was I going to get Sir Steven—or any of the attractive extras and make-up artists he employed—to even know who I was?

Well, I didn't have a name but I did have a role. I was the robot cook, draped in a faded white uniform with a small cook's hat tilted on my head. Thus, when Spielberg examined each character in full wardrobe the day shooting commenced he paused upon seeing me.

After we all formed a single line so he could inspect us like a military general reviewing his troops, he carefully surveyed me. Spielberg took special note of the left half of my face which was covered by a metallic mask and the underlying make-up. It took two hours to apply and belied the story line of a robot cook being burned in a kitchen fire.

Seeing my two hooks, now robotic contraptions, the director said, "You have two of those. I'm impressed. But I don't even have a name for you in my script."

"Sure you do," I replied smiling under my caked-on cosmetics, "I'm the Robot Cook. But you can call me Cookie."

The man who had garnered billions of dollars in movie sales yet still wore a dingy bomber jacket and dusty Yankees cap laughed. "I like that," he said. He turned to his assistant. "Make sure you put Cookie in the first scene tomorrow."

From that point forward, Spielberg ate a lot of catered Krispy Kremes and, due to liking the arms, make-up, and *sass,* used a lot of Cookie.

THANK YOU, SCOTT DELGADILLO

My ninth principle is directly related to the sixth one, and really, a by product of remaining committed to leaving a place better than when you first found it.

Impact Your Community

To some that will sound simple and to others it will seem near impossible. If the directive to impact your community sounds like common sense, then congratulations because chances are you are already engaging in activities benefiting others.

However, if there are those wondering if one person can truly make a quantifiable difference in the lives of others, let me tell you a story. It involves Notre Dame and my life, but it is not about me nor did it take place at the university.

Approximately four years after earning my Bachelor's degree in Communications, I was content living back in beautiful San Diego. My lifestyle consisted of working hard in sales and marketing for the Hispanic Chamber of Commerce during the week, devoting my autumn Saturdays to watching Notre Dame Football, and spending Sundays either basking in the glow of a Fighting Irish victory or lamenting a tragic loss. Every game, it seemed, was a life and death matter and I had no problem pinning my happiness on the scoreboard results of helmeted young men.

One afternoon in September 2000, I received a phone call changing that perspective. Not immediately, but gradually and unquestionably.

On the other end of the telephone was a representative from the local Make-A-Wish Foundation. Familiar with their mission of granting wishes to terminally ill children, I did not need too much background information as they explained they were assisting a 14-year-old boy battling cancer.

I figured perhaps they were calling upon the Hispanic Chamber and me because the young man was named Scott Delgadillo, clearly of Latino descent. Then when I heard his wish was to visit the University of Notre Dame and attend a football game because, like me, it was his dream school. I realized they were hoping our local alumni club could help too.

Putting the Make-A-Wish workers in contact with the Notre Dame Club of San Diego was a quick task and when the club arranged for Delgadillo to fly to South Bend for a late September game between the Irish and Purdue University, I figured my work finished.

When game day arrived, I convened with the members of the alumni club so we could engage in our usual religious passion of rooting on our alma mater. However, one club member arrived with a greater degree of excitement.

Shari Cassingham showed up for the game bursting with pride. Her son, Shane Walton, a San Diego product, was recruited by Notre Dame to play soccer and now successfully walked on to the fabled football team. Shari's enthusiasm on this day, though, had nothing to do with her son earning a starting role as a defensive back.

Shari told us that, in realizing his dream of visiting Notre Dame, Scotty got to meet head football coach Bob Davie (who took over when Holtz left the school). He so impressed Davie that Scotty was asked to speak at the Friday night pep rally before a crowd of 12,000 fans.

Scott Delgadillo did not hesitate and delivered such a heartfelt, unprepared speech on the importance of cherishing life and making the most of every day that the crowd gave him a thunderous standing ovation. Shari's son, Shane, was so moved that he sought out his fellow San Diegan and promised Scott two things: he would intercept a pass for him the next day and would stay in touch as Scott continued his battle with cancer.

You can imagine the emotion and awe the next afternoon when Shane Walton intercepted a pass thrown by superstar quarterback Drew Brees (who later would be drafted by the San Diego Chargers) and returned it 60 yards for a touchdown.

Nice story, right? I thought so too and figured it would be the last I'd hear about Scotty Delgadillo.

However, Shane made sure he kept in touch with Scotty, who then contacted Shari, who then asked if I would consider visiting Scott. Thus, on a gleaming star-filled night I journeyed to Children's Hospital with my buddy Adriana Holguin, also an N.D. alumnus, to visit Scotty.

There we saw his vigor and the unmistakable definition of courage. Bed-ridden and undergoing several painful chemotherapy treatments, Scotty nonetheless was convinced of beating his disease. He didn't allow us to speak about his challenges, choosing instead to focus on crucial topics, like the role of the option quarterback in the Notre Dame offense.

As fall blended into the holiday season, Scott and the entire Delgadillo family became close friends with Shari, Shane, Adriana, and me. We were inspired by his constant passion for life and, further illustrating the power that we each have to impact others. Just as he said he would, Scott got better and was released from the hospital.

Then, on a bleak winter morning in early 2001, I received the phone call I dreaded and hoped to avoid altogether. After a rollercoaster battle of health and illness, with ups and downs, remissions and releases from the hospital, followed by sudden sicknesses and returns to his doctors, Scott Delgadillo died.

It was tough, knowing that he wouldn't graduate from high school and attend Notre Dame. Whereas previously my priorities were so screwed up that I considered a football loss to be defined as "tragic." I now knew the meaning of that word when I looked into the eyes of Scott's parents Carmen and Henry, and his younger brother Eric.

Scott was honored with two funerals, one in San Diego and one at Notre Dame, which was presided over by Monk Malloy with Shane Walton and several teammates serving as pallbearers.

However, from death springs life and from adversity and tragedy spring hope and renewal. The Delgadillo family embodied this by first taking time to grieve and then they regrouped. When the time felt right, they announced their plan to create an organization called the Friends of Scott Foundation (FSF). This foundation provided emotional and financial support for families with children battling cancer.

Scott's parents emphasized that the financial

drain was as much of a burden as the emotional one. Sixty percent of the patients in the Children's Hospital Oncology Unit were Latino with parents who spoke little to no English. Thus, when she asked if I'd serve on the FSF Board of Directors, I was both humbled and honored.

I never imagined I'd be involved in such a cause, helping to promote joint fundraisers with the San Diego Padres, or touring the Children's Hospital facilities to meet families facing this overwhelming challenge. Fortunate not to have lost a close family member or friend to this disease, my perspective was skewed to where work, sports, and nightclubs were my primary focus.

Scotty changed all that. I knew him all of five months and his glowing smile, thirst and zeal for life, and the way he did things like go room-to-room to encourage the other patients in his unit, changed my outlook. He made a lasting impact on my life. Looking back, I am still moved by the thousands of pep rally fanatics he inspired in his impromptu speech—many of whom wrote him letters to tell him so—and the thousands more who were equally inspired when his devotion to life and Notre Dame was chronicled in both the *San Diego Union-Tribune* and *South Bend Tribune*.

One young man impacted thousands of people.

The power of one is a tremendous force.

We each have this opportunity. Often we are bogged down in our work, goals, and objectives and we lose sight of life as a precious gift. We lose sight of treating each other with kindness and appreciating those in our midst. Lost too is the opportunity to do something meaningful to improve the lives of others.

Without question, life is a struggle. It can be at once tedious, difficult, and easily consumed by the mundane. Frequently we focus on the chores of work and home life and the pursuit of pleasures in our social lives. Each is important and balance is crucial. Nevertheless, additionally we should take time to reflect on the greater meaning our lives hold. Specifically, what we can do for others.

Scotty knew his time on earth was short, though there is no doubt in my mind he truly intended to whip his cancer forevermore. Nonetheless, with the grim possibility his death was only weeks or months ahead, he squeezed the most out of every day. He counseled and encouraged other patients, many older. He prepared himself so whether he was answering a letter writer or journalist, or making a pep rally speech at Notre Dame's Joyce Center, his comments were motivating and purposeful.

Thanks to his family, Scotty continues to impact others through FSF. We should all take time to consider how we may leave lasting impacts like Scotty.

God supplied each of us with talents, expertise, and even a level of caring which can be applied toward the betterment of lives.

Volunteer. There is no shortage of talent within us nor is there a shortage of people who need our help. That just may be the true meaning of the Great Audition: what did you do with your abilities and talents and how did you help others?

I am proud to say I am involved with Rotary International, a worldwide organization hosting weekly networking breakfasts and lunches. However, its primary objective is not to grow your business, but to expand your opportunities for community service. They host leadership camps, fund international health and education missions, and emphasize integrity in business dealings. The Rotary Four-Way Test intention is to help you self-monitor your words and actions. It consists of:

- Are your comments true?
- Are they fair to all concerned?
- Will it build goodwill and better friendships?
- Will it be beneficial to all concerned?

Of course, there is a high level of fun and constant laughter during Rotary events. Do you think I'd belong to a boring group who took itself too seriously?

I was inspired to join Rotary because they sponsored a camp called RYLA, which stood for Rotary

Youth Leadership Awards. I attended as a high school student in my junior year, the one in which students make decisions which impact the rest of their lives. I return to RYLA every year as a speaker and possibly get more out of this energizing weekend than the students do.

This is a fraction of what Rotarians do and I love being a part of an organization dedicated to service. Rotary International has a mantra of "Service Above Self."

Scotty Delgadillo reminded me of the importance of such groups and that we can each impact our communities. We need not be famous or rich to accomplish this, just dedicated. We should not live and depart this earth without leaving a legacy.

RETURN TO COLOMBIA

There are the personal sacrifices others make *for* us allowing us to be in the position to make sacrifices ourselves. In this country of colossal opportunity, where would we be without the men and women who die in uniform protecting our freedoms? Or the fire and police officers risking their lives daily as they safeguard us? When you consider women and minorities did not always have the right to vote, should not the same gratitude be extended to those who died so we may enjoy that essential democratic right?

However, there is one sacrifice we have all benefited from, though invariably it comes in different circumstances and histories: the sacrifices of our parents.

Whether brought up by both or one parent, or if the one/s that raised you were not your actual birth parents, there is a level of love and sacrifice you received as a child that you may not fully comprehend or appreciate. No one can grasp the sacrifices a parent makes until that child is an adult, and no one can grasp that love until the adult has a child of their own.

Parents make sacrifices of time, energy, and money—most of which we will never know because they would never admit to it. Whenever I make a speech, particularly to youth of any age, I emphasize they need to thank their parents and also people who are past or present military personnel. Without them, kids would not be sitting there listening to me or anyone else. You might think this is greeted with a rolling of eyes, but invariably there is a wave of heads nodding and smiles.

Adults think their offspring never listen to them, but they do. It just takes a few years for the message to seep in past the natural tendency to be stubborn. Take it from a former knucklehead who, when I started my first job and commenced paying Uncle Sam, told my mom, "Now I know what you always meant about saving money and being careful with credit cards. I don't know how you fed all our mouths and paid taxes at the same time. Thank you for doing the impossible."

This leads to my tenth principle. You can live a life of incredible wealth and prosperity, but it is not truly a life of excellence or fulfilled relationships unless you have this critical component: gratitude.

It should be directed toward your parents, peers, or mentors who made sacrifices made on your behalf.

Show Your Gratitude

Thank your teachers for steering you in the right direction, send notes to your mentors—particularly if you cannot see them often—keeping them posted on your daily progress, and show your parents you are grateful for how they raised you by simply calling or having weekly meals together. This may sound far too obvious to some, but truthfully, there are those who are so driven in their pursuit of excellence that they forget to show gratitude to the people who put them in the position to succeed.

In those cases, you can live a life of prosperity but not true excellence because an extraordinary life contains fulfilled relationships.

This principle is also imperative in showing gratitude to those who make our everyday lives easier. If you can name every high-level executive, administrator, or professor in your building or school, but do not greet the secretaries or janitorial staff, yours is not a life of excellence. Personally, I am not as good at remembering names as I would like, but I make an effort to say hello to the support staff of a working environment. Why? Because as both my mom and dad would say, "You gotta take care of the people who take care of you."

To that end, showing your gratitude can also extend far beyond the security guard, cook, or maintenance worker. My parents set a fantastic example by being generous with tips or holiday gifts for those who worked diligently yet often went unrecognized. However, they also made certain when it came to those we knew well, say relatives or friends, that we showed them gratitude as well.

Birthdays were always the most opportune time for this. A birthday was not just a reminder that someone aged another year but a genuine opportunity to celebrate God putting them in our lives and to thank them for being who they are. Friends often laugh at my somewhat encyclopedic memory of birthdays and anniversaries, but that's how I was raised; to treat those days as more than just an occasion for cake and beer (which do actually taste good together). It's an occasion to show gratitude for one's friendship and to truly demonstrate that excellence and love are ingredients in your daily life.

Besides your parents, mentors, friends, and military veterans, there is someone else you must show gratitude toward: yourself! Part of enjoying an extraordinary life is showing *yourself* great gratitude.

You deserve great credit. No one else on this earth has your identical personality, and no one has more potential to influence our world than you. Likewise, the reason you have many of the adversities you face is because somewhere in the divine plan you were chosen to handle your particular challenges.

So give yourself credit. You're absolutely unique; you're one of a kind. Thus, be good to yourself. Give yourself options whereby you can succeed in life. Take care of your body. Give yourself rest; something overzealous people deprive themselves of in pursuit of excellence. Look out for yourself before you look out for everyone else. I am a huge believer in taking time out for yourself. When possible, splurge on yourself whether through a shopping trip, vacation, or favorite activity.

Of all of these principles I identify, none will be achieved unless you take time for personal inventory. That is, you need to take time out and ask yourself, "are you living a life of excellence?" "Who are your mentors and what adversities are you facing?" "How do you defeat them?" "What are your dreams and ambitions?" Many of us are like hamsters running in those little wheels inside their cages, moving furiously but going nowhere. Take time off the merry-go-round of life and take stock of your vision, challenges, progress, and most important relationships.

For me this is done often on long jogging excursions, where my thoughts are lost amid the breathless jaunt on a gorgeous sunny afternoon. Stress gets relieved, frustrations are driven away, questions are brought to the forefront, and even if problems are not immediately answered, I've thought them through. Plus, no one's going to confuse me for a member of the United States Olympic relay team—I like to slow my jogs into brisk walks and take a few minutes of rest. It is there, on a concrete bench or patch of soft grass, that I take inventory of my life and where it is going.

Whether you prefer jogging, walking, or just sitting still, and whether the environment is a bustling city, scenic park, or tranquil beach, take time for yourself. Consider how your life has developed in the past year, month, and week and establish a plan for how the next equivalent time frames will contain goals of excellence and fulfilled relationships.

You also owe it to yourself to truly get away from your everyday concerns. The most fulfilling activity I took part in at the University of Notre Dame was a spiritual retreat called the Notre Dame Encounter (NDE). There is nothing more powerful or, I believe, important than retreating into nature to enjoy God's stunningly beautiful creations and sorting out your life. This is why I still participate in the alumni version of NDE, called Vocare—derived from the Latin word for vocation, which we all must seek out—and the annual Rotary Youth Leadership Awards camp in Idyllwild, California. This amazing weekend camp is where I met my speaking manager and book publisher, Jim Ponder, a fellow Rotarian who embodies the ideals of Service Above Self. Jimmy will agree if you cannot take an occasional weekend to enjoy nature and "retreat into the wilderness," as I like to call it, you are in big trouble.

Make no mistake, showing yourself gratitude can occur in other places as well. Be willing to treat yourself to a vacation or a frolic-filled trip every few months and don't let cost impede you—no matter where you live there are plenty of opportunities for even a low-budget road trip. Some people enjoy tossing their money aside in Lost Wages, Nevada, and others enjoy visiting The Big Apple, Hollywood, or my majestic favorite, Miami. Whichever city, state, or country you choose, you owe it to yourself to travel—and to regenerate your mind so that it is geared toward excellence. The key is to get away.

Let me tell you about a trip I embarked upon in October 2002 encapsulating every aspect of sacrifice and gratitude of which I write.

I left Medellin, Colombia at the age of four. In that span, in addition to my two elder siblings, my parents had a baby girl, whom I knew only through our frequent phone conversations and correspondence.

Growing up I was determined to return to Colombia. As maturity came, I also had a far better appreciation for the sacrifices made by both of my mothers and vowed to return to South America to show that their efforts were not wasted.

In the fall of '01 another miracle and example of generosity allowed that vow to be fulfilled. In the 18 years since my visit to Colombia, I had not seen my parents except through occasional videotaped messages. They knew I matriculated at Notre Dame and I knew they were proud. But because they did not see me grow up, they did not know how and what I had grown to be.

In November of that year, all that changed. My older sister from Colombia, Elizabeth, wrote a letter to talk show host Marta Susana, whose television show was broadcasted in both North and South America. The loquacious Susana, who was a chain-smoking ball of energy with spiky bleach-blonde hair, invited viewers to submit letters asking for specific holiday wishes. My elder sister penned a letter detailing the fact that my family in Medellin had not seen me since 1984 and she had a request.

That must have really made Susana puff on her smokes because, one afternoon, my phone rang and an associate producer on the other end was inviting me to Florida. I was told that my sister contacted them, and a wish was being granted. Once I was convinced this was not a prank, I agreed. "Wonderful!" the producer replied. "Your flight leaves tomorrow!"

Fortunately I was able to delay the trip—a whole whopping day and off I went.

When I arrived in Miami, I still did not know what *The Marta Susana Show* was going to do. However, I had my suspicions—and hopes. After being cloistered in a hotel overnight, the following morning I was whisked away to the television set of the show. Patiently I waited backstage, listening to Marta give introductions and then I heard a familiar voice. A voice I heard countless times over the telephone, but whose face I had not seen for almost 17 years. "Alejandro, come on out here," Marta shouted. As I stepped out, I heard loud cheers and then this woman rushing toward me.

"Alejandro!" My sister exclaimed, hugging and kissing me.

Then Marta explained this was not the only surprise. What I did not know was the producers sent a camera crew to Medellin. Marta directed me to look at the screen behind me. It was my mother. And she was saying how happy she was that I was coming to see her. *See her?* The reason I was coming was because Marta Susana asked Avianca Airlines, the leading company for United States-to-Colombia transportation, to donate a round trip for me to see her and the rest of my family.

Even after the show was filmed and I was surveying the fiery sunset on Miami's South Beach, the

truth sunk in: the following autumn I would be fly-
ing to see my mother for the first time in 18 years.

The months leading up to October 2002 were
filled with explaining to people why I had two mothers: One who gave birth to me and allowed me to
leave Colombia because the United States offered
me greater opportunity. The other raised me and
instilled lifelong lessons and characteristics.

That person entrusted with raising me was my
mother's sister in San Diego, who became my mother
as well. That's the one I call Mom, Mama, and
Mamita. She is the most incredible person I know
because, not only did she take me in, she reminded
me of the need to update my mother on all my life
events.

Similarly, I had the same relationships with my
fathers, or as the old sitcom was called "My Two
Dads." My birth father was in Medellin, though
when I visited there in '02 he was on a temporary
visa in Atlanta, Georgia where he worked for several months before returning home. The man who
raised me, Frank Callahan, was the one I addressed
as Dad and when he and my Mom divorced he still
remained in that role.

As the time neared, I reflected on how the
United States was my home. My only real memories
of Colombia were of people staring at my prosthetics. As I looked around, I realized I was going to

miss my family here. San Diego was home to Mom, Frankie, and my sister Ann Marie, who though was technically my cousin, was truly a sister to me—and best friend.

And I was spoiled with drive-through burger joints, reality television and the Fighting Irish Football telecasts—luxuries I doubted I would find in Colombia.

When the day arrived for my trip, I internally complained of the lengthy route I was taking. Separate plane flights from San Diego to Los Angeles to Mexico City to Bogotá to finally Medellin. Every flight meant new pairs of eyes were glued to me.

I was tired and cranky and wondered why Marta Susana ever arranged for this trip.

As I disembarked, I searched for my mother. A sea of faces, which one was Mama—my Colombian Mama. But every mother knows her child, and my mother knew me. She remained calm as I fell into her arms and soaked her small shoulder with my tears.

How utterly selfish and foolish I was with my complaints! Every mother wants the best and more for her child and since Ines had one that was born with a disability, she was even more compelled. She knew what the United States offered. This was the woman who surrendered me to a richer life. Now at

28, I could show my mother her sacrifice allowed me to become a self-sufficient, independent man.

It was a whirlwind month, seeing my last remaining grandmother who sadly passed away eighteen months later. The one who worried what would become of me. Cousins popped out of every corner.

It was delicious, as was the Colombian steak, beans, and beer I devoured daily. In my family's apartment, I'd wake up to a breakfast of a hot buttered tortilla called an *arepa,* sprinkled with salt and enjoyed with hot chocolate or juice. Afterward I'd prepare to shower, to which my mother protested, "You can't leave anywhere yet, Alejandro. We have lunch to eat!"

Thankfully, I too adored Colombia. It had made gigantic leaps since I'd last visited, and now had an elevated metropolitan train system, flourishing businesses, and people scurrying everywhere on taxis or motorcycles. The internet had as large of a presence as it did in America—meaning I could email my friends and follow Notre Dame's undefeated football team online—proving it truly was a World Wide Web. Also, my family moved into a nicer neighborhood, where people seemed more enlightened and stared at me less.

I invaded the dance floors of Medellin's finest nightclubs, and fell in love with more than one Colombian beauty—which is redundant, really. I saw a few guys—who I noticed always wore mismatched colors, like donning a purple Minnesota Vikings cap, blue L.A. Dodgers jacket, and red Chicago Bulls sweatshirt. Plus an amazing sight: motorized wheelchairs. Now this was progress!

I attended my cousin Claudia's *quinciñera* in celebration of her 15th birthday.

And it was at Claudia's party I truly knew why I came. Not to party or drink beer, though fun. Now in her mid-50's, my mother did not move around as well after some surgeries. But she had a secret desire and my relatives shared it with me. So as the music started up, I rose and walked up to my mother.

I reached for her hand. "Mama, may I have this dance?" Leading her across the dance floor, holding her tenderly, but securely, I trusted she knew my heart as all mothers do.

Rain pelted the Colombian streets that night, but inside the salon there was warmth and gratitude. A lifetime of it.

SPIELBERG. GWYNN. LESSONS.

I t happens to me nearly every day.
    I am asked to a party.

I am invited at PETCO Park in San Diego, at the movie theatres, at restaurants, at bus stops, in airports, in churches, and while jogging down the street on Saturday mornings.

Constantly requested to partake in these huge, elaborate parties; people are convinced I'm happy to be invited.

But I'm not. Because they're not the type of parties involving great food, upbeat music, or cheerful celebrations.

They're Pity Parties. And chances are you've been invited to one too.

A Pity Party is what I call it when someone tells you your problems are so severe you can't possibly overcome them. They're not giving you empathy, they're giving you sympathy and there's a major difference.

Empathy is showing concern and relating to one's

plight. Sympathy is feeling sorry for someone to the point where you give more credence to their troubles than to their ability to overcome them. People think they're being kind and compassionate when they say they are sympathetic to your concerns, but really, they are de-valuing you. They are focusing more on your adversity rather than your ability to conquer it.

I'll never forget standing in line with my family at Disneyland—a place so happy I've visited roughly 25 times—when I was about seven. A lady approached me and made a statement that was like the floppy-ear hat she wore: Goofy.

"Oh my," she blurted out upon seeing me, "I feel so sorry for you!"

I wasn't sure if perhaps my Mickey Mouse ears looked silly, thus causing her consternation, but Mama quickly responded.

"Why, because of his arms and leg? That's non-sense," my mom replied. "He is perfectly normal. I feel sorry for *you*."

I felt bad because the lady was seemingly well intentioned. But only a few days later someone else walked up to us at Alpha Beta—remember that grocery chain?—to say nearly the exact same thing. Mama was patient with them though I thought she was going to sock them with a loaf of bread.

People saw me and instantly were struck with pity. They just assumed I must lead a life of misery and hardship. But in truth, pity was never part of my vocabulary. It certainly was a non-existent term at home, where I was given no special treatment. That made me look at myself for what I really was—a normal kid.

The reason pity was never allowed in our home was not only was it ludicrous to wallow in that emotion when things got tough, but because we focused on an entirely different word: *Persistence.*

Excellence—Persistence Above Pity

I was not allowed to pity myself if the neighborhood boys didn't choose me for a football game or if a girl turned me down because she didn't want to be seen with a guy with hooks. Now don't confuse that with uncaring. My family let me cry, vent, complain, and shared my pain. They were always there for me. But the difference between those who throw pity parties and those who live as champions is champions know when pity parties need to end.

My family was made of champions who wanted to see me become one too. I cried and lamented all my frustrations, but once I got it out of my system, they knew it was time to end the pity party and throw away the streamers. Every frustrating incident was followed up with a game plan of what I was going to do next to pick myself up.

If a girl rejected me, what could I do to make

the next girl—and they knew with me there would *always* be a next girl—see past my arms and get to know my personality? If a kid who didn't know me decided to call me Captain Hook what could I do to make him my friend—or respond with a better comeback? Hey, my family was not trying to raise a saint, they just wanted to show me some choices to illustrate that I was the one with the power, not anyone else.

Pity was not tolerated. I am glad it wasn't because truthfully people just assumed I would be downcast in life.

I've even had people tell me, "I think it's so amazing how you get around. That must be so tough to do. I feel so sorry just looking at you." True story! They think they're giving me a compliment!

Hardships surely arise. But my parents and siblings taught me every challenge was a triumph just waiting to happen.

The same goes for you.

It all starts with attitude, with being grateful for what you have and not letting your challenges overwhelm you. Then you add the crucial element of being persistent. You don't have time to feel sorry for yourself about being jobless if you are immersed in job-hunting or getting yourself trained. You don't have the energy to feel sorry for yourself about being turned down by that boss or that paramour if you're out there looking to improve yourself.

Tough things happen. We all encounter moments of harsh treatment and even cruelty. But what matters in life is not what happens to you, or what kind of hole you're in, but how you respond to it!

It's perfectly fine, and even healthy, to allow yourself to get gloomy and mourn a certain loss or tribulation. But then what? Will your pity party be a one-day affair or a lifetime of despair?

When I talk about persistence, I mean that in a few different ways. Persistence is a multifaceted word.

In my personal challenges, it meant not giving up whenever a simple task—like opening a door or unbuttoning a shirt—turned into a long and grueling activity. However, there are times when you try something a million times and fail a million times. If you try a million more times, all you'll have is two million failures. They say a sign of persistence is being willing to bang your head against a proverbial wall as a sign of not giving up. But sometimes, all you get is a headache.

That's why persistence does not mean necessarily trying the same things over and over. Be flexible and if you are chasing a dream that has resulted in multiple rejections, don't be afraid to try new approaches.

There are times when you must adopt the phrase *"work smarter, not harder."*

Persistence doesn't mean doing the same things over and over, it means trying new ideas or techniques yet never losing sight of your goal.

I also believe persistence means putting one's self in a position to succeed. If you are seeking a coveted job, submit your résumé and inquire about the opening. Be creative in showing your interest and willingness to work hard. If there are networking events you know your hopeful boss will be attending, approach him/her to get important "face time." If possible, develop a correspondence with them—much easier to do now via email—and do not be afraid to promote any special programs, events, committees highlighting your talents.

Persistence in this regard means not being afraid to stand out. And you'll never stand out if you hold back and simply wish.

Put yourself in a position to succeed. Make your name known and your reputation synonymous with credibility and success. I tell people, especially youngsters, success is never just handed to you. You have to pursue it and you pursue it by giving yourself a fighting chance. You'll never win an election unless you run—sometimes multiple times—and often times you'll never get noticed as a singer, actor, or musician unless you perform over and over so you can be noticed by that one talent scout who can skyrocket your career. Like a team striving to win a Super Bowl or World Series, you can't win the championship unless you reach the playoffs first. *You've gotta be in it to win it.*

If you are intent on making the most out of life, you must remain persistent in your desire to live as a champion. Persistence is more powerful than pity. Persistence can help you through tough times every time they return—and they do return, for all of us.

After you have determined not to let obstacles get you down, there is a further requirement in living a life of overcoming: living in excellence.

Then there is living that life of excellence. Because after achieving your dream, how will you live it? Often I ask myself if I am living in excellence. Am I demanding the best of myself?

Which is the next principle:

Live a Life of Excellence

Sitting not on a plush leather couch but on a hard wooden bench in a domed arena, which once housed the massive ship the Queen Mary, I saw I had not fully demanded excellence of myself. Because I saw who did and he sat in the director's chair with the name *Spielberg* emblazoned on the back.

Forgive me if it appears as if I am name dropping because it truly is not my intention. I am blessed to have met individuals who are well-known and have influenced me greatly. They are distinguished because they gain international acclaim for doing something with great superiority, and they gain superiority from demanding excellence of themselves.

This leads us to Steven Spielberg again. In creating AI, the entire cast, even us robots who had no speaking lines, were instructed to report to the set every day at 6:30 am. This was to eat breakfast, have our make-up applied (for my Cookie character this was an hour-long process), and get into costume in time for the eight o'clock start. Sure enough, at eight o'clock Spielberg rolled onto the set in one of his many Jaguars or other sterling automobiles, wolfed a Krispy Kreme, lit a cigar, and had camera in hand.

I learned more from watching this man in a span of two weeks than I did from many professors over the course of four years. Some lessons were instantaneous and reflective of personal character. For example, Spielberg, multi-millionaire, was never late, never wore anything fancier than a faded leather jacket and ball cap, and made it a point to greet every single member of the cast, crew, and his assistants.

Despite having legions of assistants eager to please and to be of service, he never asked us to do anything he wouldn't do himself, be it on time or stay late. (Cookie appreciated that.)

In fact, he remembered Cookie and greeted me with a hello and bantered about how his Yankees swept my Padres in the 1998 World Series.

Observing Spielberg whenever I was on break—which in the film industry is frequent and makes the day actually tedious—was to witness a true purveyor of excellence. He came to work prepared, knowing what each scene called for and correcting any mistaken actor or assistant director without ever needing to look back at the script. His legion of assistants insisted they could relay messages for him or command a crewmember to adjust a faulty piece of the background set, but he often knelt—on a set completely filled with sand—to fix it himself. There were millions of dollars in sophisticated cameras available, but he envisioned each scene by placing both hands, sometimes around his eyes and sometimes in a mock square a few inches in front of him, to capture how he wanted a scene to look.

What I remember the most is the repetition. Lines, scenes, action shots all repeated until he was satisfied. However, it wasn't mere egoism or hardline tactics driving him. What stood out was several of his minions pleading, "We can film these last shots on our own. They're simple. Go home. We'll take care of it and you can come back tomorrow at 10."

However, Sir Steven would have none of that.

He oversaw every shot. It wasn't that he was a mania-cal workaholic—he once told an assistant his kids have constant access to him and he could avoid traf-fic jams by having a helicopter airlift him home, true story—but rather he just demanded excellence in every shot. Not only that, but he wanted to *be there* to ensure *we were* demanding that of ourselves.

This man could have phoned it in on most days but exhibited the work ethic of a starving graduate student filmmaker. His margin of error he allotted for was the size of a postage stamp, but it wasn't through angry words or tirades by which mistakes were cor-rected. It was through the words "Do it again."

To Spielberg What was Important Now was getting it right—even if we truly hadn't gotten it wrong!

I appeared in approximately one scene in A.I. and the entire 2.5 seconds I am on screen you see all of Cookie's back, but not my face. But I learned so much that eight months later I accepted Spielberg's casting agency invitation to be an extra for one day on his next film *Minority Report*. (There I saw Tom Cruise and realized how much we look alike...from the neck down. True story.)

Excellence is something demanded of our-selves and those around us. It requires persistence, patience, repetition, humility, and high standards. It entails not being satisfied unless whatever you and your team are outputting is not merely good, but great. It is identifying something you love and dedicating countless hours to it. It is also identifying something—at any stage in your life—and saying you love the craft so much you will not just be good at it, but great.

It was evident Spielberg had a copious attention to detail and that he'd identified filmmaking as a love during his youth. All of his projects were products of excellence. He probably reminded himself of that commitment to excellence each time he embarked on a feature film. I don't know, but his actions indicated as such when we were leaving the set at nine in the evening and returning nine hours later.

I accomplished a dream by appearing in two of Steven Spielberg's films, but they brought me neither fame nor wealth. What they brought me was a new standard by which to measure personal excellence, and the knowledge all of us have the potential to achieve this in our lives.

I love sports. I am enthralled by the competitiveness, the majestic feat of an athlete at the top of his or her game, and the cooperation necessary for teamwork to thrive. I am riveted by the fact you never know what might occur during any given game and the whole foundation of sports is, whether it's an individual competition or a team sport involving a round ball, there's no telling where those bodies or that ball will go. The results often produce stunning, even emotional and spine-tingling memories lasting a lifetime.

If you want to read about humankind's failures, open up the front page of a newspaper. If you want to read about our triumphs, go to the sports page.

Determination. Perseverance. Goal-setting. Emotions. Passion. Overcoming adversity. All of these are discovered daily through athletics.

I once heard the head basketball coach of Duke University Blue Devils make a statement on television on which you can literally base your life. After a devastating loss in the 1998 national championship game to the lightly regarded University of Connecticut Huskies, a reporter asked Duke's head basketball coach if he was crushed.

The revered Mike Kryzweski, known to the masses simply as Coach K, responded calmly yet firmly, "No. I'm not crushed. You see, the most important thing in my life is the relationships I have. After tonight, the relationship I have with my players and their families is still intact, if not stronger. I don't live for wealth or fame or even championships. I live for relationships. So tonight, I'm disappointed and I hurt for my players. But I still have those relationships."

Coach K probably gave for free in one statement for what therapists and self-help books charge hun-

dreds of dollars. Relationships are the most important aspect of life. Not many expect that revelation
coming from the sports world.

I recall my first foray into professional sports as
an usher. Remember Gugs who hired me? He knew
he had a real opportunity to impact how fans were
treated when they attended a Padres game. Though
he was quickly ascending to a vice president's role
within the organization, he knew hiring and training the ushers was one of his primary responsibilities, and he wanted to go above and beyond what
was expected of him. Thus, he sought to increase the
diversity of the ushers—including hiring more persons with disabilities—better reflecting the community members greeted at ballgames. He then changed
the job title from usher to Fan Service Representative. This later was revised to Guest Service Representative when the team moved into a new venue,
PETCO Park.

It reflected an entirely new attitude that "Gugs"—
as he preferred we call him so Guglielmo would not
seem so imposing—implemented. Enhance staff
diversity, elevate the job titles, and blend it with
annual training emphasizing superior customer service. As a result, Major League Baseball consistently
ranked the Padres #1 in customer relations. Eventually Gugs was assigned to other vital responsibilities
and had laid the groundwork for his successors. His

firm commitment improved his department and his staff.

Sports also produce a spirit of achievement few other fields can match. One athlete instilled in me a commitment to live in excellence akin to Lou Holtz's fiery instructions.

Allow me to illustrate one further encounter.

In San Diego, no professional athlete is as beloved as San Diego Padres outfielder Anthony Keith Gwynn. By the time Mark Guglielmo hired me onto his game day event staff in 1999, Tony Gwynn had already played for the Padres for 17 years. I spent my entire life watching him line base hits to left and chase fly balls in right field with an aggression belying his portly physique and creaky knees.

But it was not until that first year as a Padres event staff employee, which required me to report to Qualcomm Stadium three hours before game time, that I fully appreciated Gwynn. In helping to prepare the ball yard for the thousands of fans soon arriving, I observed Gwynn and learned the definition of demanding excellence from one's self.

Over the course of an eventual twenty-year career, Gwynn amassed a .330 batting average, eight batting titles, and 16 trips to the All-Star Game. He broke records set dozens of years earlier and late in that '99 campaign, recorded his 3,000th career base hit—an automatic credential for the Hall of Fame.

When it came to team accomplishments, he was the catalyst for all three of San Diego's trips to the postseason in 1984, '96, and '98. The 1984 and '98 clubs made it all the way to the World Series. Yet it was evident that a year removed from his last playoff participation, this Padres club was going nowhere in October.

Still, there was one man who arrived to the stadium daily as early as the groundskeepers: Tony Gwynn. He was the lone figure swinging in the batting cage in the early afternoons and the last to reach the player's parking lot at night. By mid-August, the Padres were so far out of contention they needed a telescope to see first place.

It was obvious that the club was not only adopting a losing formula, they were selling off expensive players in exchange for younger players they could groom for their new downtown abode. In other words, that losing formula was something that was going to stick around for four more years.

Yet Gwynn persisted, treating each game like it was a precursor to the playoffs and practicing like some kid was about to take his job—which no one was. Finally, one day, when I received an assignment to work in an area near the player's locker room, I had to ask him about this apparent obsession to be a great hitter on a terrible team.

Knowing Gwynn's appetite for food was as ferocious as his appetite for hits I enticed him with a candy bar—true story—and let him ask questions about my arms as he chewed. Event staffers were instructed to not converse with players just as Spielberg also told his extras to not say hello to Tom Cruise, but, of course, I was going to talk to T-Gwynn!

So I asked him, "What drives you? What makes you so hungry to succeed after all these years?"

Maybe I shouldn't have used the word hunger because he asked for more chocolate of which I had none, but Gwynn was more than willing to respond. He threw his head back and chuckled as his first few words came out, which also made his belly jiggle.

With his voice sounding like a country boy pinching his nose, he said: "Alejandro (the name on my pin), that's what it's all about. If you ain't doing something in excellence, then why do it?"

He went on to explain that in the 1980s he was one of the first players to videotape his at-bats and his wife Alicia helped him study and analyze the footage. Teammates thought he was crazy for lugging this recording equipment on road trips, but, for Tony, excellence meant studying his craft in minute detail. He then followed up those study sessions with early trips to the ballpark for hours of practice—including days off.

This resulted in the eight batting championships. Yet Gwynn was not satisfied. He knew where he lacked the most skill was in his defense. So to be an excellent player he spent countless more hours on drills pertaining to catching and throwing. This led to several Gold Glove awards, baseball's highest defensive honor, which Gwynn rated as his proudest achievement because of the required effort.

Gwynn's explanation was, "You need to find something you love and commit to being the absolute best at it. This means hours of study, sacrifice, and never being satisfied. Anything short of that is disrespecting yourself and your craft."

What was fascinating too was Gwynn was also pitied—seriously—by colleagues who said he was underpaid by not playing in a large media market. But Gwynn chuckled at that recollection and said it was absurd for people to actually pity him for playing the game he loved. He then noted that in 1987 he had lots of adversity in his life—and still won the batting title.

Why? Because of one word: focus. He focused on his craft and his desire to be the best hitter ever. He was committed to excellence—and detail—like Holtz and Spielberg.

So many people focus on their shortcomings and challenges instead of focusing on excellence. A commitment to excellence is something we can all strive for, no matter what our trade is. Anything less is an insult to your ability.

I deeply respect Tony Gwynn. He defined what we should all pursue: excellence.

Where will excellence take you? Perhaps to PETCO Park—located on Tony Gwynn Drive.

HUMOR ME

It's all about attitude. It's about trusting God. He equipped you with the tools to succeed. And most importantly, it's about looking inward and realizing it does not matter what you may be missing, as long as you have faith in what you have. For me this meant not worrying or being hampered by not having all four limbs. It meant utilizing my full left leg along with my love of learning, writing, and communicating. I have faith. I have family. I have friends. I even have prosthetics enabling me to type on a computer, play soccer, and play the role of Cookie, the burnt robot chef. I need little else.

Except for one more critical asset.

You may not succeed in life, nor overcome personal challenges, if you are serious all of the time.

I lean on my faith, friends and family, and relentless desire to live an extraordinary life. But there is another critical pillar that has guided me in overcoming my obstacles: a sense of humor. In defeating your barriers and challenges, remember:

Keep Your Sense Of Humor

Oscar Wilde once said, "Life is far too important a thing to talk seriously about."

Humor is one of your most powerful weapons. It is as important as your intellect. A sense of humor will help you to see the levity in otherwise frustrating situations.

One of the main ways I kept from ever getting too down or negative was through laughter, and seeing the humorous side of even my most daunting challenges. As mentioned earlier, I'm not above gag jokes, *"Boy, this dinner cost me an arm and a leg!"* When I was younger and still growing into my prosthetic leg, causing a severe limp when I walked, I dubbed myself "The Pimp with the Limp." Mama won't like that, but it made my challenges seem less overwhelming and also relaxed those around me— especially those who didn't know me well enough who hadn't learned yet I preferred barbs and jokes over their respectful silence. I always said my closest friends were the ones who were not afraid to make fun of me. If it was good-natured then they were treating me as an equal, which is all I ever wanted.

A strong sense of humor also helped me to turn tough situations around into positive ones.

For example, one year in college a brutal winter storm invaded South Bend, dropping the temperatures to *sixty below,* including wind chill. Of course, it was coldest in the early morning and it just so happened I had an eight o'clock class. How cold was it, you ask? It was so cold the weather forecasters warned any exposed piece of flesh could freeze over and if you sneezed, icicles would grow out of your nose. True story. Well, part of it.

Because of the cold, I knew the classroom building, DeBartolo Hall, would be ridiculously overheated. This meant for those of us with four eyes our glasses would steam up more than a sauna. Still half-asleep, I prepared to combat my fogged-up lenses by wiping them before I entered the building. To do that I needed to flip my left hook, which merely required me to push my hook against my lip.

Except...

My lips' natural warm moisture, the hook cold from freezing temperatures...

Think of a sizzling summer afternoon, a frozen lime popsicle, your wet tongue!

Think bonding.

Unlike a hot day, however, this was not going to melt.

Moaning, I stood there, as frozen as the weather—while my spectacles continued to fog up. Unless I wanted to spend the rest of my life with a hook as a mouth, I had to do something. Squeezing my eyes shut and taking a breath, I let it *rippp*—no pun intended.

Meanwhile my friends were in hysterics.

I wanted to cry, but the tears would have turned into glaciers. Cry-me-a-river would be cry-me-an-igloo.

However, it was more than that. This occurred during a tough stretch when I was not convinced I could endure the rough curriculum, and the lifestyle and the weather. I was at a point of giving up and this was almost the last straw.

It only took scant minutes for word to travel about my frozen emergency. Some were in disbelief but most of my pals laughed uncontrollably. Here I wanted sympathy and they were doubled over in laughter.

Which then made me laugh. It was a vivid reminder of the fact that humor makes our challenges easier to endure. Really, it is as vital as remaining strong-willed and committed to living an extraordinary life. A good sense of humor is integral to maintaining a positive attitude.

As the illustrious writer, Chamfort put it, "Of all days, the day on which one has not laughed is the one most surely wasted."

It's all about how you look at life. Are you going to wallow in self-pity over your challenges or are you going to empower yourself with a strong faith, circle of friends, and laughter?

Frankly, the most frustrating aspect of my disability is it often takes me longer to do the simple things others may take for granted. I am blessed my health is not compromised or have daily physical pain like so many others. My challenges are often a series of smaller limitations and frustrations. I was trapped in a room for hours once because I couldn't grasp the slippery round doorknob. Again, that is nothing in comparison to the challenge others face, but it can be maddening.

However, what is more empowering? Getting angry and down over a slippery doorknob, or laughing about it and sharing the tale at happy hour later? (Of course, installing a rubber grip or a lever on the doorknob is even better.)

Once, before a business meeting in a government building, I knew before entering the hallway I had to walk through the metal detector. Anyone who travels with me will attest this can be a harrowing experience. I show my hooks to the security guard so they know the alarm will go off as soon as I pass through, and inevitably, once the alarm sounds everyone within ten miles looks and points. That's after guards draw their weapons.

On this particular day in sunny San Diego, the guard, an older female, calmed everyone who looked over as soon as I set off the alarms. She then asked me to step aside, grabbing a hand-held scanner, to which I warned, "I also have a prosthetic leg."

I forget whether her name was Peggy, Margie, or Gladys, but I distinctly remember her uttering something about a hand check. To which she put down the scanner, and with her right hand patted down my arms...fine...my legs...no problem...but then kept patting. All I could think about was that I was late and had to get into my meeting. Suddenly I felt a firm clenching of my gluteus maximus, to which Security Guard Gladys bellowed, "Well I can see that ain't part of your prosthetic!"

How terrible. How humiliating. How funny.

I was ready to sue Gladys, the County of San Diego, *and* Governor Schwarzenegger! True story.

Humor and comedy can be uplifting and essential to overcoming your challenges. You don't think God has a sense of humor? Think again; it's all about how you look at things. If you consider your challenges to be burdensome and stifling, they will be. But if you see the lighter side of things and consider your tribulations may actually be ironic and humbling—the ingredients of a good joke—you will be empowered.

Of all my public icons—Cesar Chavez, Dr. Martin Luther King Jr., Michael Jordan, and Steven Spielberg—I would most enjoy a dinner with the late, great Bob Hope. He often said he was neither handsome, elegantly voiced, or a tremendous actor. Yet he appeared in hundreds of films, shows, and televised specials, crooned on radio and stage, and appeared in every type of role imaginable. He knew, above all, he could make people laugh. Did you know that the Library of Congress has over a *million pages* of just his one-liners?

He did not deliver fiery speeches or even many inspirational quotes. He brought laughter and comedy and with those, a sense of empowerment. Few ever lived a fuller life than Bob Hope.

Humor is powerful.

THE LOVE BOAT

One of the most frequent questions I get asked is if it's tough for me to land a date or romantic encounter.

Truthfully, my pickiness, for which I am notorious among my friends, is the largest obstacle in that area.

But that doesn't mean there are not hurdles or heartbreaks.

My first girlfriend was when I was a love struck 16-year-old junior at San Diego High School. Veronica was a cheerleader with flowing chestnut hair, almond eyes and a serene smile.

We met when I accidentally bumped into her in a school hallway. After one glance I made sure we accidentally bumped into each other every day for the next week.

I appreciated that we could talk, laugh, and share. She was completely at ease asking questions about my arms and most of the time didn't even want to talk about them anyway. She was purely interested in *me*.

But only a week into our relationship, I noticed one gray May day Vero appeared troubled.

"What's wrong?" I asked.

"Oh nothing."

Even as a teenager, I knew when a girl said it was nothing, it was always something.

So I persisted. "You can tell me. What's bothering you?"

Veronica hesitated, and then finally sighed, "It's my friends on the cheerleading squad. They say I shouldn't date you...that maybe I should look at other guys...and...and it hurts me because I want them to like you!"

"Oh. Is it my personality? Am I annoying? Do I tell too many jokes?"

"No, they like your personality. They think you're nice."

"What is it then?"

"It's your arms...I mean, you don't have any arms...I mean...oh man. They just think dating a guy with prosthetic arms is bad for my reputation and as a cheerleader I should be dating a football player or something."

A bolt of disappointment flashed through me. "Uh, I see. Hey, that's cool. If you need to stop seeing me..."

I couldn't believe I gave up so easily, however it seemed to be the right thing to say. However, before I fully absorbed what I said, Veronica's voice rose. "Forget it! They're the stupid ones. Who cares what they think? They're not even true friends anyway. I'm with the best guy on campus, and that's the only thing that matters."

Relief blended with pride swelled within me. Despite the admonitions of her "friends," Veronica stuck with me.

Our relationship did not last too long as school-work consumed both of us, preventing time together. But I always remember Veronica, my first girlfriend, and the way she looked past any physical differences and focused on the person on the inside.

Then there was "Melissa." Yes, this is an alias.

She was two years younger than I yet seemed unflappably mature. Melissa was gorgeous, with dark coffee-colored hair extending to her waist and doe eyes. She had the type of pretty face stunning in its simplicity—no make-up needed, save for a hint of eyeliner.

After knowing her for several months and chickening out of asking her to Homecoming or the Valentine's Day dance or any number of group outings to In-N-Out Burgers, I'd finally had enough of my cowardice. After all, I was the guy who a few years earlier wrote an amorous note to a young lady, only to watch her dunk it in a nearby trash receptacle with the authority of Shaquille O'Neal. True story. It didn't really scar me; if anything, it made me ask what did I have to lose this time.

So I mustered up some bravado and asked Melissa to my senior prom. I was quaking, but she was characteristically calm. And sweet. The best part was she said yes—on one condition.

I had to meet her parents first and get their permission.

Seemed a little matrimonial to me, but I said sure. How hard could it be?

I was all set to visit Melissa's household after school. As soon as the last school bell rang, I trudged toward Melissa's abode.

Melissa's family lived in an area called Barrio Logan, which translated means "Logan Neighborhood." But the "Barrio" part stuck because the neighborhood is distinctly Latino.

To get there I hopped on a bus that departed from my school's downtown campus, and within 15 minutes I was on the outskirts of downtown. Though the two regions were separated by only a few miles, there was a stark difference as cosmopolitan shops and restaurants were replaced by graffiti-scarred buildings.

Many of the houses were converted into storefronts, with homemade signs touting *Fresh Tamales or Tax Preparation / Preparacion de Impuestos* inside. Most of the *tiendas* advertised bilingually: milk/ *leche,* bread/*pan,* and beer/*cerveza.* Because so many Latino immigrants, from all Latin American countries, routinely sent money to assist relatives in their homeland, signs for payment-wiring services were abundant.

I glanced at my watch to ensure I wasn't late. Melissa had left a half-hour earlier and told me while I was finishing up a layout meeting for the school newspaper; she was going home to get things prepared. What she had to prepare I was unsure. Last minute dusting? A bountiful feast? Hide her father's shotgun?

All I knew was that perspiration was dripping from my temple.

As I shuffled past a bevy of alleys, auto-repair garages and shops specializing in Mexican party goods—*piñatas,* streamers and *dulces* (candies)—it occurred to me that this was the type of neighborhood people reputedly wanted to avoid. Certainly, like most big-city areas, and maybe even small-city ones, it was not wise to travel there at night, especially not alone. You can say that about a lot of places, irrespective of locale.

But it seemed unfair that Barrio Logan would be labeled as unsafe when each store, church or home-based business seemed to focus on one thing: family. Walking through a Latino neighborhood, you're bound to hear two things wafting through the air (itself filled with the aroma of food): music and the sound of kids playing games.

This devotion to family is a staple of Hispanic communities and is one of the reasons many stay in the same barrio for many generations. *Abuelito y Abuelita* bought a small house there, had children, and now see their grandchildren running about on the same street. Your grandparents' friends did the same thing, and everyone's families spend 40 years getting to know each other. On any given day in the *barrio,* one's house may be visited by friends, cousins, uncles, aunts and others.

Melissa's household fit that description. It was teeming with activity as I walked up, with boom boxes blaring classic mariachi songs as youngsters kicked a soccer ball in frenzied fashion.

Squeezed onto the porch to greet me was a gaggle of whispering kids who Melissa shooed aside. I suddenly felt nervous about giving her the traditional peck on the cheek as ten pairs of eyes were watching intently. On that wooden porch, through the screen door and into the house, a flurry of introductions commenced with people whose names I'd never remember, save for Chuey and Esmeralda. Chuey is a common nickname for guys named Jesus (pronounced hay-soos), and the Latino populace is full of exotic names like Esmeralda. I don't remember if they were cousins or friends, but no doubt, they were all in the same.

In a narrow hallway, walls were covered with family pictures and crucifixion depictions, with prayers in English and Spanish.

A side room was filled with older men, uncles probably, who were watching a news broadcast *en Español.* Their brows were furrowed, and they tugged nervously at their mustaches, looking away only long enough to politely greet the visitor in pressed jeans and a floral button-down shirt whom Melissa had introduced. After hand shaking and names again tossed about, my beautiful young lady quickly whirled out of the side room, waving off whatever for urgent news.

Two electric fans hummed through the arid hallways. From the back of the house, where the kitchen was located, music was piping through a small radio. The two most important people for me to meet were there. One was standing over a stove, and the other was cleaning some type of tool or appliance at the table: Melissa's parents.

"Mamí, Papi, quiero presentarle mi amigo Alex," Melissa said. After wiping their hands with an apron and rag cloth, respectively, Mom and Dad shook my hand, nodded in a friendly manner and said, "Hello."

That was the general extent of our conversation that afternoon. They spent the remainder of the day speaking in Spanish. Even when their offspring chimed in with English phrases, the parents still responded *en Español*. Often in Southern California, you'll hear a mixture of both tongues—Spanglish—and families will alternate languages the way they do dinner menus.

Speaking of food, Melissa's *madre* prepared a scrumptious dinner. Carne asada, beans, tortillas and thick rice.

It was good that my mouth remained filled because language was a barrier. As a native Colombian who moved to the United States at age 4, I was considered a *pocho*—a term for one born in the United States who identifies more with this country than that of his cultural heritage. Language is usually the largest factor in pinning someone with this label and my Spanish was not polished. Exactly ten years later after my return visit to Colombia and with years of schooling and working in an environment where Spanish was frequently spoken, I was far more confident. But in the spring of '92, I understood more than I could speak.

Fortunately, Melissa's parents were more interested in speaking than in listening. Sure, they asked all the standard questions about my interests and family and this impressive school in South Bend to which I had just been accepted, but I had rehearsed all those answers and had my Spanish-speaking friends modified my grammar.

Really, they weren't as interested in the preciseness of my responses as they were the overall likeability of my character. Was I respectful to them and their daughter? Did I listen when they relayed stories about growing up in Baja California? Did I sway to the *rancheras* when the volume was increased on the radio dial?

They didn't even say a word about the prosthetics taking the place of my missing arms; their attitude made my prior nervousness on the subject unworthy.

Regardless, I must have done all these things in suitable fashion because, though no formal announcement was declared, Melissa smiled as she guided me to the screen door at dusk.

"You better catch the bus to your house before it gets dark," Melissa noted.

"But did they..." I stammered.

"Don't worry," she said. "You can pick me up next Friday at 7."

So I made the cut!

Except...

Melissa turned out to be a terrible date.

By terrible I mean wayward. Turns out, she arranged for another guy she liked to meet up with her at the dance. Since he came stag, she requested—ostensibly out of kindness—to take a picture with him and enjoy the first slow dance with him. I relented, and two hours later, my date was canoodling with Rico Suave near a staircase.

Her loss though. She missed out on the chance to be seen on stage with the Prom King.

A GOOD CITIZEN

Over the course of seven years, my daily schedule consisted of work at the Hispanic Chamber all day long. Then I would hop on the trolley and work on the game day staff of the San Diego Padres. On Sundays in the fall I also ushered Chargers games at Qualcomm Stadium. I could have worked San Diego State Aztecs games too, but did not want to give up my passion for watching Notre Dame Football.

Quite frankly, it was a grueling existence. Handling a busy public relations job, followed by a five-hour stint—mostly standing, with one half-hour break—was tiring. But I loved the baseball environment and I knew it was what I wanted to do full time. I kept my eyes on the prize.

As an usher, I got to see the behind-the-scenes action of Padres baseball. How hard the Entertainment Department worked to keep fans engaged. How tirelessly the Community Relations staff worked to make the dreams of kids come true by introducing them to their favorite players. How many people arrived to work early, long before the first pitch, to set things up and how long they stayed afterwards.

Because I am a huge believer in networking and "face time"—the belief nothing is more effective than meeting face to face with someone and developing a relationship—I kept working with the Padres. I got to know people within the organization and the better I knew them, the more I saw that the club's values matched mine—community activism, generosity, and sports as a platform for good works.

The more they got to know me, the better they knew my skill set and interests. Thus whenever a job opening arose, the club was good about informing me and encouraging me to apply.

So I did in 2002. I thought I'd be good in Marketing.

I interviewed but didn't quite make it.

Both times I heard similar decisions:

You're doing good things and you're very talented but it's just not a good fit. Plus for these positions we really need someone with more sports business experience.

Keep at it, someday you'll be here.

As encouraging as they were, and though the interviewers raised good points about a certain amount of experience needed, the turndowns still disappointed. And as positive as the decision makers always were, I was just not sure if I'd ever get there.

I also didn't want to appear desperate either. But I knew sports management was my desired destination and as Mama repeatedly said, "It just isn't your time yet. God must have something better planned for you."

Meanwhile I focused on a concurrent lifelong dream: becoming an American citizen.

I was eligible to apply after five years of legal residency, but then things got thorny. In order to complete an application for United States citizenship, one had to submit fingerprints.

I stared at my hooks. Fingerprints?

I sent a letter to the then-Immigration and Naturalization Services explaining.

Rejected.

My doctor wrote a letter verifying my usage of hooks.

Rejected.

Finally one morning I marched into the downtown INS office. There's nothing like doing things up close and personal.

The lady at the registration desk examined my case files and saw the "DENIED" stamps and looked up with a puzzled expression. She then asked, "Well why..." before glancing at my arms. "Ohhhhhh!" she said.

Promised a waiver, I trusted I was on my way.

Incredibly, I received another letter two months later.

Application Denied.

Enough already.

I contacted my local Congressman, Bob Filner (D-CA), known also by the humorous moniker *The Joker* due to the permanent smile on his face. Upon learning of my rejection three times for being unable to submit fingerprints, Filner's perpetual grin was erased.

He and his staff member Manny Doria in San Diego wrote letters and kept phone lines buzzing between California and D.C.

"Darn it, Alex," Filner told me one day, "it's just not right. All this is red tape and we're going to cut through it. If I can't fight for people like you, why did I get elected in the first place?"

True to his word, Filner doggedly pursued my case.

About six months later, I received a letter: "*You are invited to take the requisite exam for citizenship with the United States of America.*"

I hooted as I had with my Notre Dame acceptance letter. It was one more hurdle, one more test, but it was finally an opportunity to gain citizenship in the greatest country in the world.

WELCOME TO THE BIG LEAGUES

Miniature flags waved and hollers were loud. It was mid-July 2004, twelve years to the month I fought off deportation and earned permanent United States legal residency. Through the tenacity of Congressman Filner, I also broke through the bureaucracy, denying my citizenship application due to a lack of fingerprints. Finally, I was granted the opportunity to take the U.S. citizenship exam and, upon passing, received notice that I was eligible to become an American citizen.

At Golden Hall in downtown San Diego, a massive auditorium used for election-night festivities and graduation ceremonies, throngs of people gathered. According to the official at the front door who registered me, there were 999, to be exact, receiving citizenship that day.

I felt the spiritual presence of my Heavenly Father, even in a rather inside-joke kind of way. Seven is a treasured numeral for me. Biblically it's called a "golden number" and I was born in the 1970s, on

6/8—7 being the digit between those two—and my legal residency and now citizenship were both awarded in the seventh month. My last name has seven letters. When I walked into Golden Hall, I asked the registration official which row of seats was I assigned. He handed me a card which each participant needed to enter the ceremony. Row seven.

Sitting there, I thought of all those who brought me to this point: My mother in Colombia, who relinquished the right to see me grow up in order for me to have a better life. My aunt who became Mom and pushed me to focus on what I had in life instead of dwelling on what I was missing. I sensed my teachers, mentors, friends, and, just as important, the people who told me my physical challenges were insurmountable—all of them driving and motivating me.

The 999 citizens-to-be spanned the globe. The presiding judge, before enlisting us to take a mass oath, did a roll call of every native country represented. Alphabetically he called out names of countries, each punctuated by cheers and delirious waving of American flags. Africa...Denmark...Egypt...Iran...Iraq...Netherlands...United Kingdom.

Every name he called elicited rousing cheers. When he bellowed, "Colombia!" I stood with probably a half-dozen other Colombians in the room.

After all countries were announced, the judged

asked us to stand. Solemn silence descended as we lifted our right hand and in unison swore:

I hereby declare, on oath, that I absolutely and entirely renounce and abjure all allegiance and fidelity to any foreign prince, potentate, state or sovereignty, of whom or which I have heretofore been a subject or citizen; that I will support and defend the Constitution and laws of the United States of America against all enemies, foreign and domestic; that I will bear true faith and allegiance to the same; that I will bear arms on behalf of the United States when required by the law; that I will perform noncombatant service in the armed forces of the United States when required by the law; that I will perform work of national importance under civilian direction when required by the law; and that I take this obligation freely without any mental reservation or purpose of evasion; so help me God.

"Welcome to your new life as an American citizen," the judge proclaimed. Everything was quiet. Then half a second later, *Yeah* resounded through the auditorium! Clapping! Whistling! A thunderous sustained roar. Waves of red, white, and blue.

My heart swelled. I was an American.

A few months later, I participated in another ceremony. This time it was an awards function hosted by the California Council on Humanities (CCH).

This literary organization promoted creative writing and the voices of writers capturing the immigrant experience. My Hispanic Chamber coworker, Candy Urreola, nudged me to enter a contest the CCH sponsored on writing a letter back home describing life in the Golden State.

I did so, describing in my essay/letter much of what I have described to you: my life spent in the greatest state of the greatest country in the world. A state and country that cared not as much about my limitations as a triple amputee but more about my potential as a writer, student, and professional. A state and country allowing me the opportunity to dream previously unfathomable dreams. I went to Notre Dame. I carried the Olympic Torch. I acted in two Steven Spielberg movies. I effected change for people with disabilities.

I won the grand prize.

"Don't get a big head," Mom told me. "Besides, the best is yet to come."

Maybe Mama is clairvoyant. Or more likely she just knows the American immigrant ethos of perpetual striving, herself being a Colombian immigrant overcoming cultural obstacles, language barriers, and the raising of multiple offspring with disabilities.

But she somehow knew. She knew of more triumphs to enjoy.

And I did.

A short time later, the San Diego Padres announced they were creating a position called Director of Latino Relations, a role intended to both outreach and market to the burgeoning Latino baseball fan base on both sides of the US-Mexican border.

Mama said, "Go for it."

The application and interview process was long and arduous, and seemingly interminable.

But anything worth having is worth waiting for. Between my first Padres job interview and my most recent one there were ten years. In that span, I sought four openings and faced four declinations. I did accept a part-time event staff position, in addition to my full-time work at the Chamber, because it provided two things: access to baseball and opportunity.

I met the right people. I learned and studied the system. I focused on what I had, not on what I was missing. I embraced new mentors. With each assignment I tried to leave the place better than as I had found it and in training new staff, attempted to pass the figurative Torch.

On March 5, 2006, the Big Leagues called—the Padres. An organization which cares deeply about its community, and to which I share a reciprocal affection, offered me the Director of Latino Relations position.

Over the telephone, I told my would-be supervisor, Jenifer Barsell, "I gratefully accept."

After hanging up, my mind, dizzied with emotion, shot back to 1984. The Padres won their first ever entry into the National League playoffs and Major League Baseball World Series. The team critics who disparaged them as small and incapable of overcoming its challenges proved them all wrong. That day the Padres clinched the pennant, the *San Diego Union* raised a banner headline on its front page. In homage to deceased team owner Ray Kroc, who died just months earlier and used this line in building his McDonald's franchises: "*Dreams Do Come True.*"

They do, Mom.

And the future is brimming with promise.

My mother, Inés Montoya González, and I took this picture before our first visit to the United States in 1976. I was two.

Before joining the Padres front office in 2006, I was an usher for the team for seven seasons. Here I am with two other game-day event staffers in my "rookie" season, 1999.

I enjoy giving public presentations about the Padres and how
to live life as a champion – things I am passionate about. This
presentation was in the fall of 2007.

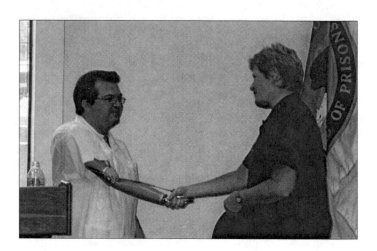

November 22, 1993

Dear Alex,

Thank you very much for your letter. You are a great person and always an inspiration to me.

We feel bad about our loss on Saturday, but the players have done a tremendous job and had a great season.

Best wishes to you, and continue your great attitude.

Sincerely,

LOU HOLTZ

ks

I have always admired the wisdom of ESPN analyst Lou Holtz. This was a letter he graciously wrote to me while he was head football coach at the University of Notre Dame in November 1993.

The work ethic and lessons imparted by Hall of Famer Tony Gwynn have always resonated with me. This is "Mr. Padre's" statue at beautiful PETCO Park in San Diego.

At the same time that I ushered during Padres night games, I worked for the San Diego County Hispanic Chamber of Commerce from 1999-2006. Our staff truly applied the principles of giving personal attention and creative problem-serving to the Chamber's cross-border membership of nearly 1,000.

Earvin 'Magic' Johnson's zest for life has always shone through and I was fortunate to meet him when the Super Bowl came to San Diego in 2003.

One enjoyable element of my job is introducing fans to the
legendary "Spanish voice of the Padres," Eduardo Ortega.

Alex Montoya is the Director of Latino Relations for the San Diego Padres. In that role he is responsible for the team's outreach and event coordination to the Latino fan base in San Diego County and Mexico. It is an area Montoya knows well after seven years with the San Diego County Hispanic Chamber of Commerce. He is also involved in motivational speaking about issues pertaining to success, education, and overcoming disability obstacles. Montoya is a 1996 graduate of the University of Notre Dame and will receive his Master's Degree in Sport Management from the University of San Francisco-Orange County in 2008.

CPSIA information can be obtained at www.ICGtesting.com
Printed in the USA
LVOW07s2233170315

430990LV00012B/206/P